A PORTRAIT OF

Rivalry

A PORTRAIT OF

Rivalry

An Untold Story

DOUGLAS G. WATERS

ARCHWAY
PUBLISHING

Archway Publishing books may be ordered through booksellers or by contacting:

Archway Publishing
1663 Liberty Drive
Bloomington, IN 47403
www.archwaypublishing.com
1-(888)-242-5904

Because of the dynamic nature of the Internet, any web addresses or links contained in this book may have changed since publication and may no longer be valid. The views expressed in this work are solely those of the author and do not necessarily reflect the views of the publisher, and the publisher hereby disclaims any responsibility for them.

Any people depicted in stock imagery provided by Thinkstock are models, and such images are being used for illustrative purposes only.

Certain stock imagery © Thinkstock.

ISBN: 978-1-4808-0136-3 (sc)
ISBN: 978-1-4808-0138-7 (hc)
ISBN: 978-1-4808-0137-0 (e)

Library of Congress Control Number: 2013913053

Printed in the United States of America

Archway Publishing rev. date: 9/18/2013

To Judith Ellen,
without whom this book
would not have been written

Contents

Chronology

├ 1738: John Singleton Copley is born in Boston, Massachusetts; Benjamin West is born near Philadelphia, Pennsylvania; the future King George III of England is born in London.

├ 1753: Copley receives his first commission and begins his artistic career in Boston. About the same time, West receives his first commission and begins his artistic career in Philadelphia.

├ 1760: West arrives in Rome.

├ 1763: West arrives in London.

├ 1765: Imposition of the Stamp Act in the American colonies.

├ 1766: Copley's *Boy with Squirrel* is exhibited at Society of Artists in London.

- 1768: West is introduced to King George III and gains royal patronage. The Royal Academy of Arts is founded in London by royal charter.

- 1772: Patience Wright, the 'wax lady', arrives in London from the American colonies.

- 1773: The Boston Tea Party.

- 1774: Copley departs Boston for London; he meets West. Copley goes to Italy.

- 1775: The American war for independence begins. Copley rejoins his family in London.

- 1776: America declares its independence from England.

- 1777: Copley exhibits *The Copley Family* at the Royal Academy. West exhibits a painting of his family at the Royal Academy.

- 1778: Copley exhibits *Watson and the Shark*, his first commissioned narrative painting.

- 1779: West receives commission for the Windsor Castle projects from King George III.

- 1781: The war for American Independence ends, when the British surrender at Yorktown.

- 1783: Copley wins commission to paint the British victory at Gibraltar.

├ 1784: Copley exhibits The Death of Major Peirson.

├ 1786: The Greenwich Naval Chapel commission.

├ 1792: West elected President of the Royal Academy of Arts.

├ 1797: The Provis Con.

├ 1801: West's royal commissions cease.

├ 1802: West visits Paris and returns to London.

├ 1804: The Knatchbull arbitration.

├ 1808: West and the Elgin Marbles.

├ 1811: King George III appoints his eldest son Royal Regent.

├ 1815: John Singleton Copley dies. West begins to dictate his biography to John Galt.

├ 1820: King George III dies. West dies.

INTRODUCTION

This is the true, untold story of two American colonial artists, John Copley and Benjamin West, both of whom were born into humble circumstances in 1738. As young boys, they both wanted to be artists. As young teenagers, they embarked on their artistic careers. They met each other for the first time in London in 1774, where they clashed as they sought the same goals: wealth and artistic fame.

As Copley and West rival each other to achieve artistic dominance in London, colonial America is struggling to achieve its independence from England. This historical struggle affects the lives of both artists, as it does a royal prince, born in London the same year that Copley and West were born. This prince ascends the throne as King George III. His choice of favorite artist surprises. But, Time decides which of the two rivals merits ever-lasting artistic fame.

CHAPTER I

Great Expectations

John Singleton Copley, the only child of Irish immigrants, was born in July of 1738. Copley never knew his father, who died, it was said, while on a trip to the West Indies to buy tobacco for the shop he owned on Boston's famed Long Wharf. This wharf extended from the shoreline into deep water, allowing large ships to tie up and unload directly to the warehouses and shops with which it was lined.

Upon news of her husband's death, Copley's mother simply continued to operate the tobacco shop, where she and her infant son lived. When Copley was old enough, he assisted his mother in the shop and played along the wharf when he could. Although life was hard and subsistence meager, Copley's mother took loving care of him and involved herself with his education. She ensured that Copley attended Boston's renowned public schools. Their modest household contained a few books and prints, which Copley could explore.

In his eleventh year, fortune smiled on him. His widowed mother married Peter Pelham, a widower with three young children. He was a schoolmaster, painter, and engraver. Copley and his mother moved to the Pelham residence in a respectable part of Boston. He lived comfortably there with his new stepsister, two stepbrothers, and soon a half-brother, to whom he became devoted.

Peter Pelham was a caring and thoughtful stepfather to young Copley, who profited from his cultivated stepfather's tutoring. His stepfather must have recognized in young Copley his interest in art, his extraordinary artistic talent, and his intelligence. It was probably under Pelham's tutelage that Copley was made to understand the importance of studying human anatomy to draw the human figure convincingly. He made a textbook for himself that went far beyond simply tracing anatomical figures. His drawings are keyed to Latin text and translated into English.

During the almost three years before his death in 1751, Pelham allowed young Copley daily access to the activities in his studio and introduced him to his library of books and prints, as well as to his artist friends. When Pelham died, Copley received a generous inheritance. It comprised a studio, books, prints, paints, brushes, and tools to engrave the plates from which prints could be made. He put all of this to good use.

At about fifteen years of age, Copley received a commission to paint the portraits of John and Elizabeth Greenleaf, ages four and five, thus marking the beginning of his artistic career. These two portraits, both oil paintings, gave "new meaning to the term precocious." Just a young teenager with no formal training, Copley drew on his inborn gifts to depict with great skill not only the siblings' likeness, but also to convey the texture and detail of their elaborate and inventive dress. In Elizabeth's portrait, in particular, one sees a remarkable degree of sentience, that is, being aware of what is going on about her.

By age eighteen, Copley had painted at least three pictures inspired by historical events portrayed in his stepfather's prints, apparently done for his own interest and enjoyment. Remarkably, he also mastered the art of miniature painting, creating works on copper, canvas, and ivory, which is a difficult skill to master. Miniature painting scaled down every detail of the subject, sometimes almost to microscopic levels. It was achieved by using extremely fine brushes, even a single bristle. Before the age of photography, miniatures were a cherished means of having easily portable images of loved ones and others. It has been said that Copley's reputation was such that at age seventeen, when George Washington visited Boston in 1755, he sat for Copley so he could paint a miniature of him.

In Copley's late teens, Joseph Blackburn, an accomplished English portrait painter superior to all other artists who had painted in Boston, arrived in Boston. Copley competed well against him artistically and learned much from his work. When

Blackburn departed Boston in 1758, Copley, at age twenty, had become a popular and well-established portrait painter with an excellent reputation. He had also developed the skill necessary for pastel painting, another challenging art form. Pastel (in the form of pastel sticks or crayons) must be applied directly to the working surface. Pastel errors cannot be covered over the way a paint error can be painted out. Copley "had never seen a work in the medium of pastel, making his accomplishment in this medium all the more astounding." He was completely devoted to his art.

Far from Boston in colonial Pennsylvania, Benjamin West, the tenth son of Irish immigrants, was born in October of 1738, in a tavern his father operated in a small Quaker community west of Philadelphia on land that is now part of the Swarthmore College campus. Little is known with certainty about West's youth except that his education was somewhat neglected. His attention was largely directed to painting copies of things he saw, for which he seemed to have a natural talent. He borrowed art books from an English painter of portraits, William Williams, and received from him some art instruction.

Like Copley, West got his first known commission while he was still a young teenager. It was to paint portraits of a young brother and sister of the Morris family. West's portraits of *The Morris Children* make them look stiff and lacking sentience. Yet, they were painted within a year of Copley's *The Greenleaf Children*. If West could have seen Copley's portraits of John and Elizabeth Greenleaf, he very well may have admitted, at least to himself, which of them had the gift of genius. Four or five years later, West painted his first known full-length portrait of a lady: *Elizabeth Peel*. It is painted well, but almost a literal copy of a work by a well-known artist in Philadelphia.

In 1756, while painting portraits around Lancaster, Pennsylvania, West was shown a print of the death of Socrates, a famous incident from classical antiquity when Socrates chose death by drinking a cup of hemlock rather than sacrificing his principles of honest dialogue, logical argument, and belief in the rule of law. A patron of West's asked him to paint a picture of this dramatic scene, and he did. Sometime later, the Reverend William Smith, a leading Anglican intellectual and provost of the college in Philadelphia, saw West's painting of Socrates' death while he visited Lancaster. Despite its awkwardness, Smith was impressed that a teenager with no formal training could produce such a painting. He persuaded West to move to Philadelphia, which in the British Empire at the time was second only to London in wealth and culture. There, West benefited from studying the work of a number of accomplished foreign-born and -trained artists. To further encourage West's artistic endeavors, Smith prepared a course of study for him that included the study of the Bible and classical antiquity. These studies omitted grammatical exercises that would have corrected his Pennsylvania-Dutch dialect so he could speak and write the King's English properly.

At age twenty-one, West decided to go to New York City to paint portraits, hoping to earn funds sufficient for travel to Italy to study the art of European Old Masters, celebrated European artists who painted before the 1800s, many of whom were Italian. He stayed in New York for eleven months. Most likely, West's idea to travel to Italy came from his classical studies and discussions with Smith, his mentor. Very late in life, West bragged to his hired biographer that while in New York, he painted numerous portraits and for some of them earned twice the amount he had been able to earn for his portrait painting in Philadelphia. Yet, not one of the numerous portraits he alleged to have painted in New York is known to exist.

When West returned to Philadelphia from New York, a surprise awaited him. Smith had obtained from prosperous gentlemen free passage to Italy and sufficient supplemental funds for him to stay there for a time. The free passage, money, and letters of introduction came primarily from William Allen and his associates, with the understanding that West would study paintings of the Old Masters, copy some, and bring them back to Philadelphia. Allen was the richest man in Philadelphia and the king's chief justice of Pennsylvania. When West left Philadelphia to go to Italy, he is known to have painted just eighteen portraits. Notably, at the time of his departure for Europe in 1760, West had not heard of Copley, nor did Copley know of West.

In July 1760, West arrived in Rome. Seasonal conditions there aggravated various health problems from which he suffered. Consequently, during the three years he was in Italy, he lived in Rome for only about twelve months, divided over three visits. Having excellent letters of introduction, he was invited into aristocratic and religious circles, thereby acquiring social skills appropriate to courtly behavior. He also exploited the advantages of novelty, being the first American artist to arrive in Italy. He was attractive in person and dress, socially friendly, and good natured. West's occasional displays of generosity would always seem to take into account the possibility of reciprocity. He strove to attract notice and to impress. Surprisingly, West did not pursue academic training while in Italy, which in those days meant rigorous study of human anatomy to draw the human figure convincingly, as Copley had done in his youth.

During the time he was not in Rome, West visited Florence, Bologna, Parma, and Venice. In Venice, when copying the famous painting *Venus of Urbino* by Titian, a great sixteenth-century Venetian artist, he failed in attempts to achieve the much-admired glowing richness and glorious use of color for which Venetian artists were famous. Later in life he would try again, fail, and consequently suffer ridicule.

While West was busy in Italy, Copley was in Boston and well on his way to becoming the supreme portrait painter in the colonies. Fortunately, England's war with France (known in the colonies as the French and Indian War) ended in 1763, and economic prosperity returned to Boston. Increased trade through Boston's port created wealth for many Bostonians. The well-to-do wanted their portraits painted to show off their status in society and to pass down their images to future generations. By 1765, Copley, then in his late-twenties, was overwhelmed with commissions. His flourishing portrait practice was earning annually what in London was equivalent to some £900. He acquired a house on ten acres of prestigious property overlooking Boston and its harbor on what is now known as Beacon Hill.

Although Copley was living comfortably with a grand reputation as a colonial painter of portraits, he was not satisfied. He wanted for himself a grander reputation. He knew that European artists achieved the highest accolades by creating paintings that depicted historical or biblical events referred to as narrative painting, or by the rather misleading term history painting. This category of painting was considered more challenging than portrait painting, for it required an artist to create a complex composition. Also, Copley realized that the art market in the colonies for the foreseeable future would be only for portraiture. So, to achieve artistic acclaim for narrative painting that would equal or exceed his reputation as a portrait painter, he would need to go to Europe to study the paintings of the European Old Masters. He could rely on Henry Pelham, his devoted half-brother, to look after his mother and take care of his property while he was away.

His first step was to learn how his artistry might be received in London. Consequently, in September of 1765, Copley sent *Boy with a Squirrel*, a portrait of Henry Pelham seated at a table playing with a pet squirrel, to an old friend in London, ship captain R.G. Bruce, with a request that he submit the painting for exhibition at the Society of Artists in London. This society, which received a royal charter, was founded in London in May 1761 by an association of artists to provide a place for the public exhibition of works by living artists. There, *Boy with a Squirrel* was accepted and exhibited. It was highly praised by the public and particularly so by Joshua Reynolds, the dean of English artists. When Reynolds saw it, he said "that it exceeded any portrait that West ever drew."

Reynolds' comment was communicated to Copley in a letter from Captain Bruce, and it was the first time Copley became aware of a compatriot named West, who unknown to him had been painting in London since 1763. In fact, Captain Bruce's letter to Copley enclosed a letter written to him by West. It contained great praise for *Boy with a Squirrel*, and included some constructive criticism. Upon receiving this good news, Copley continued to send portrait paintings to be exhibited at the society to show case his artistic talent. Copley must have been pleased when he was accepted as a Fellow of the Society of Artists in absentia.

Over the next several years, Copley and West exchanged a few letters. Copley looked to West for assurances that he would be able to earn sufficient income in London to live there well. He was repeatedly assured by West that he could do so. Even with these assurances, Copley was still having difficulty making up his mind about going to Europe to study art when nature made up his mind for him.

In November 1769, Copley married Susannah Farnum Clarke, daughter of Richard Clarke, one of Boston's richest merchants. The firm of Richard Clarke and Sons was a major consignee of tea that came to Boston as the principal agent of the East India Company. Susannah was a beautiful, highly intelligent young woman, who had about her an aura of poise and calmness. Copley became a father of three children. His first child, John Singleton Copley Jr., was highly intelligent and good looking. He was followed by two sisters, who grew to be remarkable for their intelligence and beauty. All thought about departing America for Europe was abandoned.

Copley placed consideration for his young family above his artistic ambition to become an internationally known artist of narrative painting. His real estate holdings grew to some twenty acres with three houses, one of which he transformed into a grand residence and into which the Copley family moved. Now, settled in Boston, he chose to become involved in civic activities. He became Clerk of the Market, whose responsibilities were to maintain good order in the Boston marketplace. There he mediated commercial disputes as they occurred.

Unknown to both West and Copley, an event that would greatly influence their lives had also occurred in 1738. An English prince was born in London whose grandfather was King George II and whose father was Crown Prince, a title meaning he was first in line to become King when King George II died. However, when the Crown Prince died unexpectedly in 1751 and then nine years later King George II died, the prince, who had been second in line, ascended the throne of Great Britain at age twenty-two as King George III. No crystal ball, however powerful, could have foreseen that these three contemporaries all the same age—two budding colonial artists and a king of the greatest empire on the globe—would become acquainted in London, nor could it have seen the role that King George III would play in the Americans' professional lives as Copley and West strove to acquire wealth and artistic fame.

CHAPTER 2

Royal Problems

In 1760, the young King George III inherited an England burdened by heavy debt from being at war with France for seven years. Realizing that his country was in pressing need of more revenue, the new king directed his ministers to urge Parliament to tax the American colonies more heavily and effectively. Thus, taxes that were difficult to administer were replaced with a single tax thought to be more effective—the Stamp Act of 1765. It required that legal documents, newspapers, and magazines be printed only on imported and stamped paper from England, on which a tax would be levied.

This new tax incensed the colonists. When the king's agents arrived in Boston with large supplies of stamped paper, large demonstrations broke out in the streets of Boston. Unruly mobs badly damaged property, the imported paper was seized, and some was destroyed. During the riots that followed, a mob evicted the governor's family from their residence and then destroyed its furniture, tore down interior walls, and emptied its wine cellar. The Crown's agents were severely intimidated; many resigned from their posts. Although Copley was not a participant, he was a sympathetic observer of those events. Many throughout the colonies boycotted British goods in response to this new tax. This hurt the English merchant class. Consequently, Parliament repealed the Stamp Act, and the political situation in the colonies calmed down.

Copley described the violence that had taken place in Boston in response to the Stamp Act in his September 1765 letter to Captain Bruce telling him that *Boy with a Squirrel* was on its way to London to be exhibited. In his description of the events, he wrote: "We demolished the Governor's House, The Stamp Office, Mr. Storys and greatly damaged Capt. Hoppowells and the Secretarys Houses." In his mind, the use of "we" in his letter referred to the enraged colonists who caused the damage and not to him personally. However, his careless, although innocent use of "we" would be consequential.

Two years later, Thomas Hutchinson, the king's governor in Massachusetts, dissolved the colonial legislature and requested that two British military regiments be sent to Boston. They were. Parliament, still seeking substantial revenue from the American colonies, imposed new taxes on glass, paint, and tea. This time, Bostonians and other colonists responded by forming a broad-based political movement to oppose the new taxation. Those who assumed positions of leadership within the opposition to British taxation became known as Sons of Liberty. Moreover, since the end of seven years of war between France and England, the colonies had been able to increase their trade with other European countries and could afford to ignore British goods. Then, the British Parliament again readjusted its taxation policy. It repealed all the newly imposed taxes except the tax on tea, a greatly desired commodity, and one for which the British had a near monopoly. This action did not appease the colonists.

In Boston, the Sons of Liberty were led by Sam Adams, a cousin of John Adams, who would become the second president of the United States. John Hancock, an extremely wealthy neighbor of Copley, provided financial support for the newly established political movement. The Sons of Liberty held public banquets to recruit members and grow support for their movement. While it is known that Copley attended these events, there is no evidence that he became a Son of Liberty. Rather, he was generally respected and recognized as an apolitical voice calling for moderation. Although he let it be known that he eventually intended to depart America to study art in Europe, he nevertheless continued to accept civic responsibilities and be a good son of Boston.

In the early 1770s, after a decade of prosperity, Boston began losing trade to the great ports of New York and Philadelphia. Its large ship-building industry and overall economy declined. Wealth became concentrated in fewer and fewer families. Copley's portrait business was adversely affected as well. Fortunately for him, Thomas Gage, commander of all British troops in North America since 1763, commissioned Copley to paint a full-length portrait of him while he visited Boston in 1769. The general took it with him when he returned to his headquarters in New York and hung it in the Gage residence.

In 1771, in need of funds and having determined he could find lucrative employment in New York as a portrait painter, Copley and his wife Susannah traveled there. Mrs. Gage, a leading social luminary and hostess in that city, insisted on being the first to be painted by Copley, whose reputation as a skilled portrait painter was widely known. He painted the colonial-born Mrs. Gage in a dress that reflected the era's fascination with the Orient. She was immensely pleased with Copley's portrait of her. It is one of Copley's finest portraits. After six months, the Copleys returned to Boston with some £370 of much-needed income.

Back in Boston, Copley accepted the even more burdensome responsibilities of being a town warden. He still thought himself to be apolitical, neither one who supported the king's policies nor one who opposed them—that is, neither Tory or Whig. Then, in December 1773, two ships loaded with tea and waiting in Boston harbor to be unloaded of their cargos were permitted to dock. Copley's Tory father-in-law, Richard Clarke, by assignment from the East India Company was responsible for the security of the tea on those ships. To complicate matters, Clarke was the nephew of the much despised governor of Massachusetts, Thomas Hutchinson, who, under the king's order, collected tariffs on ships' cargos.

Sam Adams, an ardent revolutionary, saw in the situation a great opportunity to defy the king's taxation policy. He became intent to block the unloading of the tea and send it back to London without any tariff being collected. Such action would result in a direct affront to the Crown and a great financial loss to Clarke. Copley, in his role as town warden, failed in his attempt to mediate a solution acceptable to both parties. In the face of serious threats from a mob that smashed windows in the Clarke residence, Richard Clarke fled to Salem and his two sons to Castle William, a royal fortress in Boston harbor.

Adams then called a general meeting of Bostonians at which his powerful rhetorical oratory won over mass approval to have a demand delivered to Governor Thomas Hutchinson that he order the tea cargo ships to return to London without any tariff being collected. Hutchinson responded that he could not do so, since it would be against British law. With this stand-off between Hutchinson and Sons of Liberty, circumstances dictated that the only way to prevent the tea from being unloaded and a tariff collected was to dump the tea into Boston harbor.

On the night of December 16, 1773, a small, hardcore group of Sons of Liberty disguised as Indians boarded the tea ships that were docked (a third ship having docked by then) and dumped large quantities of the tea into Boston harbor. It was said to have been valued at £1,500. Thus, what became known as the Boston Tea Party bankrupted Richard Clarke and provoked an extremely punitive response from a very angry King George III and his Parliament. This was just what Adams had anticipated and wanted.

Four months later, around midnight, the Copleys were awakened by a mob at their front door. This unruly group was looking for an officer of the king whom they suspected was in Copley's house. Copley truthfully told their leader that the man for whom they were searching had been there but was now gone. After a warning to the Copleys, they left. Later, the mob returned and threatened Copley with serious harm if he were caught lying. Copley then told them that the man had been at John Hancock's house, his neighbor, for reasons unknown to him. It being near the Copleys' residence, the man stopped by to say hello and was invited to dinner with the Copleys, after which he departed. After threatening Copley again with bodily harm, the mob left. One wonders what might have happened if this officer of the king, whom the mob thought a villain and rogue, had accepted the Copley's invitation to stay the night.

This unsettling and disturbing incident convinced Copley that he was between two irreconcilable political forces, a dangerous place to be, not only for his safety, but also for his family's safety. He knew if he stayed in Boston, he would sooner or later have to choose sides, something he did not want to do. This left him with no other choice but to leave colonial Boston. It was agreed that Susannah, again being pregnant, would join him later in London with their children. That decided, Copley set sail for London in June of 1774.

CHAPTER 3

Getting There First

As unrest in the American colonies was mounting over the king's taxation policy, West was already in Italy. While painting in Venice, West met Richard Dalton, the librarian of the newly crowned King George III. It was West's first encounter with someone of significance from the king's court. Dalton was in Venice to acquire from Joseph Smith, the king's consul there, his collection of paintings, drawings, books, gems, and medals that was wanted by the young king. West learned from Dalton that the king was born in 1738, the same year as he, but in June. West probably found that intriguing. Dalton urged West to visit London at the end of his three-year stay in Italy before returning to Philadelphia, which West decided to do.

About a year later, West traveled to London, arriving there in August of 1763. While in Italy, he had copied eight Italian masterpieces, six of which he sent back to Philadelphia as promised. Thus, he arrived in one of Europe's great capital cities with just a few paintings on historical subjects and probably some on mythological subjects.

On his arrival, he found to his great surprise and delight that his principal patrons from Philadelphia, William Allen and the Reverend Dr. William Smith, were there on business. They brought West to the notice of London's Anglican Church leadership. Members of that group became his first London patrons, commissioning portraits and religious art. Two other significant events occurred soon after his arrival in London: West married Elizabeth Shewell, his sweetheart from Philadelphia. And, he exhibited at the Society of Artists two paintings of subjects taken from mythology that were probably painted while he was in Italy. These paintings, which could be considered erotic, received considerable attention, as did West, because he was the first colonial artist to paint in London. But public and critical reaction to them was mixed. Some critics hailed West as a painter of feminine beauty, while others did not. Horace Walpole, a noted author, historian, and self-appointed critic of contemporary English art, wrote in the margin of his exhibition catalogue: "These are much admired, but very tawdry," meaning sleazy, showy, gaudy, or cheap. Citro, an anonymous critic and contributor to the newspaper *The Public Advertiser*, wrote: "Until Mr. West exhibits some more striking performances than those he has already done, surely the glorious title of the American Raphael can never be without irony bestowed on him."

West somehow had managed to acquire the tag "Raphael" while in Italy and made this known when he arrived in London. It was flattering. Raphael is reputed to be one of the greatest painters of sixteenth-century Italy. One wonders whether naming his firstborn son Raphael was done to sustain this association, rather than naming him Benjamin West, Junior, as his second son would be. Ten years after his arrival in London, West painted *Self-Portrait with Raphael West* and had prints made of it. One wonders: Was that done to remind?

During his first five years in London, West painted some twenty-nine portraits and exhibited seven of them at the Society of Artists. Of those, just one produced some excitement. It was that of General Robert Monckton, the deputy commander of the British forces that defeated the French at Quebec. He also exhibited seventeen narrative paintings that figured prominently in critical reviews, that is, published examination of their merits or lack thereof. They had limited public appeal. Just three of the seventeen were engraved for sale in London's large, robust, and prosperous print market, which was supported by a large middle class unable to afford original paintings. Overall, this was not an auspicious beginning for an artist, who may have decided by then to remain in London and establish a grand reputation.

Then good luck—extraordinary luck—intervened. In early 1768 West received an invitation to dine with Robert Hay Drummond, Archbishop of York. As the evening progressed, as West recounted it to his biographer many years later, West was told a story from ancient Roman military history. It was that of Agrippina bringing back to Rome the ashes of her husband Germanicus, one of Rome's great generals, who had died under mysterious circumstances. Drummond expressed interest in having a picture of that event painted. West went home and sketched a composition he thought would be satisfactory to Drummond. It was. When West completed the painting *Agrippina Landing at Brundisium with the Ashes of Germanicus*, Drummond obtained an audience with the king, took West with him, introduced him to the king, and displayed the painting. As West recounted the tale many years later, again to his hired biographer, the king displayed a spontaneous liking for him and his painting, such that the king read to him another event from ancient Roman military history—the departure of Regulus from Rome—and commissioned him to paint it. Regulus was a Roman Consul, who gave his life to sustain Roman honor. So it was that the Archbishop of York was the ultimate and indispensable person who brought to dramatic conclusion the remarkable string of coincidences that brought the young Benjamin West from a small Quaker village in Pennsylvania to the court of King George III, then the king of the United Kingdom of Great Britain and Ireland. Take away any of the coincidences—West being asked to paint a picture of the death of Socrates; West painting the picture; Smith going to

Lancaster and seeing the picture; Smith arranging for West to go to Italy; West meeting Dalton in Venice; West following Dalton's suggestion to visit London; West's patrons Allen and Smith being in London when he arrived there; and Drummond inviting West to dinner and subsequently introducing him to the king—there would not be this story to tell.

West, a commoner from the American colonies, soon became a favorite of the king. To the dismay of other artists in the realm, West, except for portraiture, enjoyed the king's exclusive patronage for the next some thirty years. One wonders why the king so hastily gave West a royal commission the first day they met. After all, the painting *Agrippina Landing at Brundisium with the Ashes of Germanicus* that West showed the king was correctly declared "not very fine" by the critic Horace Walpole when he saw it exhibited at the Society of Artists. Nevertheless, the king was pleased and commissioned West to paint more narrative and religious paintings, to the exclusion of other artists in his realm.

CHAPTER 4

A Royal Academy

In November of 1768, the same year West met King George III, Sir William Chambers, whom the king had appointed Royal Architect, arranged to call on him. Chambers had been one of several tutors to the young George, who in his youth was given a classical education and instruction in the arts. He told the king that he, as well as other artists of solid reputation, would like to establish a society that would be called the Royal Academy of Arts. Its purpose would be to promote the arts more effectively than previous art societies had done. It would sponsor grand public exhibitions and establish and administer schools for instruction in the fine arts. This idea appealed to the king. He instructed Chambers to prepare founding documents. Chambers did so, assisted by several other future academicians, the title given to artists who were to be members of the academy. West was not included in Chambers' working group.

Having presented the idea of a Royal Academy to the king and working to found it, Chambers wanted to be its first president. In approaching the king about that, he was unaware that the king had already asked Joshua Reynolds, the dean of English artists, to be the academy's first president, an offer which Reynolds had accepted. Unwittingly, Chambers told the king that Reynolds was insisting on being given more time to consult with two individuals who were members of a loose alliance that frequently was in opposition to what the king wanted. Nonetheless, the king's trust in Chambers was such that he overlooked Chambers' ploy and named him the academy's treasurer, the only one to be a paid officer in the academy. Chambers would be summoned ex officio to all Royal Academy Council meetings, and it was he, not the president of the academy, who then served as liaison with the king on academy matters.

On December 10, 1768, through a personal act of King George III, the Royal Academy of Arts was founded. On the April 21, 1769, the Royal Academy for the first time opened its doors to the public for a grand exhibition that it called a Summer Exhibition. For some five weeks, the public, after paying admission fees, viewed art by contemporary artists. West's painting *The Departure of Regulus from Rome*, which the king had commissioned a year earlier, was prominently exhibited. The total number of pictures exhibited was 136. The exhibition room was always crowded, and even the streets outside were often impassable because of the waiting carriages with their footmen and people pressing to get in. On the same day that the academy opened its first exhibition, Reynolds was knighted and became Sir Joshua at a levee, an afternoon assembly for men held by the king at Saint James' Church. Every year following the academy's first exhibition, its annual exhibition continued to grow. By 1772, the catalogue for that exhibition listed a total of 324 works of art, including several contributions sent across the English Channel from Paris by members of the French Academy of Art. Eight years later, when the academy held its first exhibition in its new home in Somerset House, its income from that exhibition was some £1,000 greater than that of the previous year, and it was financially self-sufficient. The king's largesse had included premises for the academy; drawings, books, and antique casts for the academy schools as well as, before the academy became self-supporting, some £5,000.

The academy's founding documents provided that its body of forty academicians would be known as the Academy Assembly, from which eight academicians would be drawn on a rotational basis, to serve for two years as members of the Academy Council. The council was the academy's sole executive authority. Every two years, the assembly would elect from within itself a president, and, as needed, other officers, provided they were acceptable to the king. Any changes in bylaws required the king's approval. He reserved the right to veto elections and dismiss academy officers, should they become unacceptable to him. The president was expected to preside at meetings both of the council and the assembly, but without executive power. The only exception was if either of the two bodies would be tied on an issue. Then he could vote to break the tie.

When the list of founding artists was presented to the king, West had managed to have his name placed first on the list. This was a glimpse of West's need to be perceived as the most important or virtuous person in any activity that involved his fellow artists. As the years passed, West strove to be first in line or claimed to be the key figure in academy events when there was no factual evidence to support his claims. Such happened when he asserted that he was the key figure in persuading the king to create the Royal Academy at the grand dinner attended by fellow academicians to celebrate the academy's twenty-fifth anniversary. West persisted in talking about the dominant role he played in founding it, despite the fact that it was generally agreed that Chambers was the one who gained the king's approval, patronage, and financial support for the academy and played a leading role in all events that led to its founding. As West's puffing continued, one of the academy's most respected academicians stood up and proposed a toast to Sir William Chambers in recognition of his efforts in convincing the king to support the formation of the Royal Academy and for his hard work in conjunction with others to draw up the documents necessary for its establishment, which were acceptable to the king. This was a pointed and appropriate gesture to recognize Chambers' work to found the academy. There is no record that anyone toasted West that evening regarding the establishment of the academy.

CHAPTER 5

Yankee London Bound

*F*ortunately for Copley, the sailing ship on which he booked passage for London met with fair weather, and the long trans-Atlantic crossing was without incident. On board, he had ample time to reflect on what life in London might be like. Yet, his ever-present thoughts must have been about the security and well-being of his family, who were still in Boston: Susannah, their children, the newborn, his mother, his half-brother Henry Pelham, and his in-laws the Clarkes. The only comfort for Copley was in knowing that the Clarkes would do their best to attend to the needs of his family. Unknown to him, his new infant son was born with serious health problems.

Although concerned about his family, Copley must have wondered about Benjamin West, his compatriot. He knew very little about him other than what Captain Bruce had written in one of his letters: "West was making great progress in producing paintings on historical subjects and was a very agreeable, amiable young man." In the several letters West had exchanged with Copley, West did not reveal any personal information. He had only reassured Copley that, given his talent, he would have no problem earning a living in London. What is notable is what West chose to omit. In his letters, he mentioned nothing specific about the London art market, little about patronage possibilities, and most surprisingly, nothing at all about the well-established, exclusive patronage that King George III had bestowed on him. When Copley arrived in London, West had already accomplished a great deal.

Remarkably, when Copley left for London in 1774, he had not seen even one original painting by West. One would expect that during his nine-month sojourn to New York to paint portraits in 1771, Copley would have seen or heard about one of the many portraits West purportedly had painted while in New York. Apparently, he did not. In his detailed correspondence from New York to his half-brother Henry Pelham in Boston, an artist himself, no mention is made of any works by West.

On the other hand, West knew much more about Copley. To begin with, Charles Wilson Peale, an accomplished American painter, had been hospitably received by Copley in his Boston studio in 1766. Copley allowed him to study his paintings and even permitted him to copy one of them, a candlelit portrait. Subsequently, Peale voyaged to London, where he occupied himself in West's studio for a time prior to returning to America. He helped out in West's studio and painted miniatures, some of which were entered in the 1768 Society of Artists Annual Exhibition. Peale would have responded to questions that West would likely have asked about Copley and confirmed to him that he was painting only portraits. West had seen the half dozen or so paintings, all portraits, that Copley had sent to London to be exhibited at the Society of Artists, including *Boy with a Squirrel,* which had been highly praised. This is why West only thought of Copley as a highly skilled portrait painter. As yet, West had no inkling that Copley wanted to do more than paint portraits and would become a serious rival. Such was the situation in late July of 1774, when Copley arrived in London.

CHAPTER 6

Copley Meets West

In London, West greeted Copley with a great display of hospitality. He was invited to dine at the West residence whenever he wished during the six weeks or so that he would spend in London before going to Italy. Copley saw that West lived in grand style. His large home included an impressive suite of rooms that comprised his painting studios, and there were plans to construct an impressive gallery on the property for exhibiting his work. His domestic staff would eventually reach six. In assessing Copley, West did not view him as a competitor but simply as a highly skilled portrait painter, who would become a fashionable painter of vacant faces, referring to that class in society desirous of having lovely portraits painted of themselves.

West introduced Copley to many socially and politically prominent people, and Copley received invitations to dine with some of them. One was Joshua Reynolds; another was the very wealthy Lord Grosvenor, who was a patron of West. In addition to *The Death of General Wolfe*, Grosvenor would commission West to paint four more large narrative paintings, for which he would pay him some £1,800. West was indeed fortunate to have a patron willing to pay that amount, for in London only the very rich had regular annual incomes of some £1,500.

Together, West and Copley visited sites of artistic interest. They went first to the Royal Academy, and the next day to the Warm Room in Buckingham Palace. There, Copley viewed five paintings that West had painted for the king, one of which was a copy of his *The Death of General Wolfe*.

West had come to recognize that the public was becoming less interested in paintings that depicted events from antiquity and more interested in viewing paintings that depicted recent historical events. He recalled that in 1762, the year before he arrived in London, George Romney, a very talented young Irish artist, had painted a remarkable narrative painting of a recent historical event. Its subject was the death of a General Wolfe at Quebec, Canada, who was killed during a battle between British and French forces. Romney's painting became the talk of London because of its originality and was entered in a competition sponsored by the Society of Artists, where it was voted a significant cash prize. But, before it could be given to him, the prize money was revoked. Romney was outraged. Blaming Reynolds, who had great sway in the artistic world, he left London and took the painting with him. It is unknown what happened to it.

West, who seemed to have a good sense of the art market and a good memory, painted his version of the death of General Wolfe, the same subject as Romney's painting, which he had studied prior to Romney's departure. Since then, two other English artists had painted the same subject. Preferring to avoid complex artistic challenges in creating original compositional designs, West took the compositional ideas of these two other artists, which were relatively simple to copy, for his painting of General Wolfe. West even decided to paint it without a commission, one of the very few times he did so. Being clever and shrewd, he chose to test his sense of the art market by first displaying the painting in his studio. Viewing it was by invitation only, and gratuities were expected for the privilege. West had guessed correctly. The painting was well received by the invitees. Thus encouraged that it probably would be well received by the general public, he exhibited it at the Royal Academy. General Wolfe, commander of all British forces then in Canada, was fatally shot, having been struck by two musket balls while leading his forces to victory over the French army defending Canada. The event took place in 1752 on the Plains of Abraham, adjacent to Quebec City. The battle was the great victory that added Canada to the British Empire.

The critical response was mixed. Walpole acknowledged that West's *The Death of General Wolfe* was a "fine picture." However, he noted, "There is too little concern in some of the principal figures surrounding the dying general, and the grenadier on the right is painted too tall." Joshua Reynolds, then president of the Royal Academy, may have gotten it right when he suggested that the public success of *The Death of General Wolfe* was due much more to its subject, which aroused great feelings of patriotism, than to its art. Engraving of the picture produced huge profits in the sale of prints. It is unknown if West collected royalties from those sales. The following year, West would enjoy even greater public and financial success when he was commissioned by William Penn's son Thomas, to paint a memorial to his father *William Penn's Treaty with the Indians*.

Prior to Copley leaving London to go to Italy, West tried several times to involve him in painting portraits by offering to get him commissions. Copley declined. Understandably, he first wanted to meet more artists, size up the competition, evaluate the London art market, and satisfy his curiosity about West. No doubt, he pondered why King George III had so hastily given West, an American artist without any artistic acclaim, a royal commission upon meeting him for the first time and had bestowed his royal patronage exclusively on him. Being King of Great Britain and Ireland, King George III could have favored other artists within his realms who, given some royal encouragement, could have produced paintings that pleased the king as much or more than those painted by West. Certainly, the king with his wealth was not constrained to limiting his patronage to West, but he did for a time. Later, he chose superior portrait painters to paint portraits of the royal family.

To his surprise, Copley discovered that very little was known about West's life before he arrived in London, other than he painted some portraits in colonial Pennsylvania and had traveled and painted in Italy for three years prior to coming to London. He learned that West was in the middle of painting a series of portraits of members of the royal family. These portraits turned out to be of mixed quality, some even being critically described as cardboard-like figures. He learned, too, that West, with the king's approval, adopted the exalted title History Painter to the King, although it would not be until some six years later that he would again produce narrative paintings for the king.

It was obvious to all at court that the king found West, a mere commoner of the same age as he, to be both agreeable and amusing. West frequently visited the king during the day and even sometimes in the evening. As importantly, West passed the political test, that is, loyalty to the Crown and its policies, an absolute requirement to be a regular at court. During the few years that West lived in the colonies as a young adult, he was not known to have participated in politics in any way. When he left the colonies at age twenty-two to study art in Italy, he was a loyal subject of the English king. He had been gone from colonial America some five years before widespread protests began there against the king's unacceptable taxation policy.

It could well be that the king's favoritism toward West was based in part on a political calculation. Without doubt, the king wanted to have an empire firmly united in obedience to the Crown and may have calculated that by recognizing and honoring West, a colonial artist, the colonies would view his reign more favorably.

This calculation might also explain the king's bizarre behavior towards one Patience Wright, who arrived in London from the colonies in the early spring of 1772.

Wright, then forty-seven years of age, was a strong and unusually independent woman who had extraordinary artistic talent for sculpting human figures that appeared real in tinted wax. She was determined to become as famous in London for her artistic prowess as she was in the colonies. She had been urged to pursue her profession in London by Benjamin Franklin's favorite sister, Jane Mecom, whom she met in Boston when touring the northern colonies. Franklin was in London representing several American colonies when Patience arrived there with a letter of introduction from his sister. Soon after her arrival, she met with Franklin and then opened a fine studio in a fashionable London district. Soon thereafter, many political and military notables came to have their images sculpted in tinted wax and visit socially with others of similar rank and status. Patience chatted easily with her clients while they sat for her. It benefitted them both. For sitters, it made the time pass quickly and pleasantly, and kept them from being bored. For Patience, it was a means to learn and gather interesting news about political and military affairs. West became well acquainted with Patience, her daughter Phoebe, and her son Joseph. Phoebe modeled for West as a nymph and a shepherdess. Her brother Joseph soon became West's protégé and was the first American colonial student to enter the prestigious Royal Academy schools.

West suggested to the king that he might enjoy visiting

Patience's studio to watch her work. He did so, accompanied by Queen Charlotte. The king, apparently pleased with what he saw, and perhaps taken with Patience herself, permitted her to visit Buckingham Palace freely so that she could sculpt his and the queen's portraits, for which they sat numerous times. From time to time, Patience met privately with the king and responded to his questions about America. Probably during such meetings, Patience asked the king questions, she being a forceful woman.

In the late summer of 1773, wax-tinted busts of the king and queen were completed and prominently displayed in Wright's studio. The king's prime minister Lord North—in tinted wax—was there to greet them. That the king of the greatest empire on the globe permitted the royal busts to be exhibited in such a commercial setting is astounding. Even more astounding was that the king permitted Patience to address him and the queen as George and Charlotte.

The Wrights kept concealed from West and the king their strong anti-monarchical views. That ceased in 1774, when the king's majority in Parliament imposed the Intolerable Acts upon Massachusetts. Wright bluntly told the king that his behavior toward the colonies was shameful. Surprisingly, her outburst did not appear to have immediate negative consequences for her. When the king's coercive acts failed to bring colonial obedience to the Crown and the king declared war on the American colonies, the "wax lady" appears to have declared her own war on the king. Ben Franklin, then in France working to obtain French economic and military aid in America's struggle for independence, received at least three letters from her that were full of hostility toward the king. At the very least, Patience became a self-appointed informer, if not an outright spy, for Franklin and other American leadership figures. She used others to mail her letters so she would not appear to be corresponding with the recipients.

Patience's son Joseph Wright, who shared his mother's anti-monarchical views, became one of the leaders of a group of anti-monarchical students at the Royal Academy, who were disruptive and of concern to the king. In 1780, Joseph exhibited his first, and to be his only, painting, at the academy, a portrait of his mother sculpting: *Mrs. Wright*. When the king and queen viewed it, they were outraged. To understand why his painting was viewed as scandalous by the royal family and those loyal to the Crown, it is necessary to recall an episode in English history.

In 1625, King Charles I succeeded his father James I as king of England. The previous year, he had married a daughter of the king of France. When he was crowned, his wife, being Catholic, was not crowned. The English majority was fearful of a return of Catholicism to England. King Charles I soon encountered trouble with Parliament over religious, financial, and political issues. After summoning Parliament and then dissolving it three times, he governed for eleven years without it. After that, he attempted reconciliation with the members of Parliament. It did not succeed. When King Charles I learned that five members of Parliament were planning to impeach the queen, he acted in an unprecedented way. He entered the House of Commons with an armed guard and demanded that these five members be presented to him. Forewarned, the five escaped. The public outrage over this action caused the king to flee London with his family. This started a civil war between the royalists, who supported him, and those who opposed him, known as Roundheads. They were led by Oliver Cromwell, who pursued and captured King Charles I. He was brought to trial before a tribunal of 135 judges and convicted of so-called treason by a vote of 68 to 67. As punishment, his head was severed from his body.

In Joseph's painting, his mother is shown modeling on her lap the wax head of King Charles I, without a neck. Looking on are the tinted wax busts of King George III and Queen Charlotte, displayed in such a way as to suggest they might suffer the same fate as Charles I. Understandably, recalling the fate of King Charles I was extraordinarily painful to King George III. He admired Charles I for attempting to subordinate the power of Parliament to the rule of the king. King George III himself was attempting to accomplish that kind of rule from the very beginning of his reign.

In 1782, when the king recognized American independence, Joseph sailed back to America. His ship ran aground, the painting was lost, but he survived. The significance of his mother's activities during the war years was openly confirmed in a letter Patience received from George Washington soon after the peace documents were signed between England and America in 1783. In his letter, Washington expressed in strong terms his esteem for her. In 1786, Patience died in England, knowing that America was an independent country. West regretted the day he introduced Patience to the king. It would not be the last time he would experience such because of a Wright.

CHAPTER 7

To Italy and Return

After six weeks in London, Copley spent a week or so in Paris, and then went on to Italy. In Rome and in other Italian cities, he continued his study of Old Master paintings. Sometimes, these paintings inspired him to paint his own version of what he saw rather than just copy them, as West had done. In one instance, Copley painted his own version of *The Ascension*, Christ ascending to heaven. Gavin Hamilton, at that time the most gifted English painter in Italy and a longtime resident in Rome, told Copley he never saw a finer composition by a living painter.

In Italy, Copley met Mr. and Mrs. Izard, a couple from colonial South Carolina on tour in Europe. He painted for them a double portrait, *Mr. Izard and Lady*. When Hamilton saw that portrait, he declared Copley "a perfect Master of Composition." The Izards invited Copley to join then on a visit to Naples to view its art and then onward to see the excavations at Pompeii, which he did. During the trip, the Izards insisted on paying most of Copley's expenses. There is no evidence that West ever viewed the art in Naples nor the excavations at Pompeii, the newly discovered ancient Roman city near Naples that had been lost for centuries buried in ash and debris from the eruption of Mount Vesuvius in 79 AD. In the eighteenth century, this discovery contributed to an intense and renewed interest in the ancient classical world.

As the months passed, Copley, still in Italy, became more and more concerned about his family's well-being in Boston. Today, in a world where instant communication is commonplace, it is easy to forget that it took about two months under the best of circumstances for news to cross the north Atlantic. Consequently, Copley was getting outdated news from Boston. Of particular concern to him was that he had learned that General Gage, who was in England during the Boston Tea Party, had returned to Boston from England with four more British regiments.

When news of the Boston Tea Party reached London, General Gage had given his king very poor advice. He suggested that if England displayed firmness toward the colonies, they would become docile, more easily managed by the Crown. Unfortunately, Gage had completely misread the temper and mindset of the colonists, but the king accepted what he said and acted on his advice. In considering which of the colonial port cities to punish for daring to disrespect the authority of the Crown, thereby making it an example of the Crown's policy of firmness, King George III chose Boston, principally for two reasons: Reaction to the Stamp Act had been marked by violence and destruction of Crown property in Boston, whereas in the other colonies groups of middle-class citizens, while calling themselves Sons of Liberty, had kept the mobs mostly under control. And second, although other port cities had tossed nominal amounts of tea into their harbors, Boston had destroyed a large and costly consignment of British tea.

When Gage arrived in Boston, Parliament had passed the Boston Port Act and the Massachusetts Government Act. These acts became known in the colonies as the Intolerable Acts. Their purpose was to punish the Province of Massachusetts Bay, whose main component was Boston, for protesting against British colonial policy. General Gage, whom the king had appointed Royal Military Governor of Massachusetts, was charged to establish military rule. The civilian governor, Thomas Hutchinson, was relieved of his job. Gage was ordered to close the port of Boston to all seagoing ships to create economic hardship for Boston. He was given authority to billet British troops in private residences and to confiscate all war-making materiel. British regimental officers selected the residences in which British officers were to be billeted. Among those chosen were Copley's attractive homes on Beacon Hill. When Copley had left Boston for London, he put Henry Pelham in charge of his real estate. Thus, Pelham collected rent from the officers, became well acquainted with them, and even dined with them and the general on occasion. Consequently, the Sons of Liberty tagged him a Tory.

There is no evidence that Susannah Copley and her children were treated other than with respect by the king's officers. But, hearing that the Port of Boston was being closed to all seagoing traffic and fearing that she and her children might become trapped in Boston, Susannah promptly and wisely found passage to London for herself and three of her four children at Marblehead, an open port up the coast from Boston. Sadly, she had no choice but to leave her sickly newborn son in the care of his paternal grandmother, Mary Copley. Both women knew he would not survive a long sea passage. In fact, he lived but a short time. Susannah and her three children arrived safely in London in late June 1775.

General Gage diligently went about the king's command to find and remove all war-making materiel in the colonies. He first deployed spies around Boston, some of whom found a large magazine of gunpowder in Somerville, now a suburb of Boston. This information allowed British troops to seize some two hundred fifty casks of gunpowder and take them back to Boston. This action by the British military caused the Sons of Liberty to organize a communication capability known as the Powder Alarm. This warning system would prevent General Gage from again executing surprise raids on the war making assets of the colonists.

In April of 1775, suspecting that the colonists had large stores of military supplies in the town of Concord north of Boston, which they did, at midnight General Gage sent a British force of eight hundred men to seize those supplies in what was supposed to have been a surprise raid. In planning the raid, he even considered that his troops might capture Sam Adams, the firebrand leader of the revolt, and John Hancock, who financed Adams' rebellious efforts. Copley had painted powerful portraits of both men and was well acquainted with them. Probably King George III would become aware of that.

The raid on Concord was not a surprise to the colonists. The general had no inkling that the colonists had developed an effective communication system in the Powder Alarm. It performed very well. Learning that the British were on the march, the Boston silversmith Paul Revere, an active Son of Liberty whom Copley also had painted, galloped at night to Lexington and then on to Concord warning, "the British are coming!" (This famous incident is known as Paul Revere's Midnight Ride.) On the morning of April 19, 1775, British troops arrived in Lexington. There, colonial militiamen confronted them and fired the first shots in America's War of Independence. They were easily scattered by the British regulars, who then hurried on to Concord. Forewarned by Revere, Concord's militia became reinforced by militias of surrounding communities. To their great surprise, the British were repelled and had to retreat back to Boston. Harassed all the way, they suffered heavy casualties, whereas the colonists suffered only light casualties. From all over New England, men assembled at Boston and began to lay a land siege of the city. Such was possible because Boston was then a peninsula. The New Englanders were intent on containing the British forces to prevent them from confiscating other military supplies belonging to the colonists.

Prior to the arrival of General Gage with his regiments and the imposition of military government, the Boston population was politically a Tory and Whig mixture that lived together reasonably well. However, after Lexington and Concord, many Tories living outside of Boston moved to Boston, seeking the protection of the king's military. Consequently, so as not to be mistaken as Tory, Whigs wisely left Boston. The winter of 1775–76 in Boston is said to have been one of the most punishing that Boston had yet experienced. Boston became seriously short of supplies of all kinds. Buildings were torn down for firewood. It is said that during late 1775, only eight of thirty-five transport and supply ships that England sent to Boston arrived there.

Having reinforcements, General Gage attempted to break the siege but failed, with major losses of troops and officers. He was recalled to London and relieved of his command. He was replaced by General Sir William Howe, the senior of three generals who had arrived in Boston with British reinforcements.

An unintended outcome of Gage's action in sending troops to Concord was that it had united colonial Americans. Representatives from all the colonies met in Philadelphia and established the Continental Congress to address what to do in response to the king's actions toward the colonies. One of the first subjects it addressed was who would be the supreme commander of America's colonial military. By unanimous vote, George Washington became the commander in chief of all American military forces. He quickly went to Boston, took command of those besieging it, and set to work organizing and training the undisciplined forces he found there into a professional army. All four New England colonies came to the support of Boston. Following Washington's arrival, some six hundred riflemen from Virginia, Maryland, and Pennsylvania arrived at the siege.

The king had written to his prime minister in December of 1774, "I do not want to drive them to despair, but to submission," meaning the colonists, and he urged that there be a vigorous suppression of rebellion in all of the colonies. When that news eventually spread throughout Washington's army, his troops became enraged. Nevertheless, for a time, a military stand-off developed, since Washington and Howe apparently sensed that the cost of victory would be too high to justify pursuit of it.

However, in the early spring of 1776, after the terrible winter through which both armies suffered, the stand-off ceased. American forces had captured Fort Ticonderoga, a large British fort facing Lake Champlain at the head of the Hudson River valley. In it Washington found just what he needed to drive the British from Boston—heavy artillery and an abundance of ammunition for it.

Henry Knox, a brilliant mathematician and formerly a Bostonian bookseller, had quickly risen in the ranks to become Colonel Knox, Washington's chief of artillery. He led a hardy band of New Englanders to Fort Ticonderoga, who disassembled the artillery and packed it so the very heavy load of canons and ammunition could be transported to General Washington in Boston. It had taken Knox and his men three months to accomplish this amazing feat in the dead of winter over a harsh landscape. By the spring of 1776, the heavy artillery needed to drive the British from Boston was in place. Knox positioned it on easily defendable heights overlooking Boston and its harbor, such that he could fire on Boston without receiving effective return fire.

This situation led to an unwritten understanding between the two generals. Howe let it be known that he would evacuate all his forces from Boston, along with all others that wished to go along, while warning that if they were fired upon while leaving, he would put all of Boston to the torch. Washington did not interfere.

After about twelve undisturbed days of hastily loading his ships and waiting for favorable weather, Howe left Boston with a fleet of 120 ships and sailed north to Halifax, Nova Scotia. His fleet was jammed full with some 10,000 British troops and over 1,000 Tory citizens, and was heavily loaded with military stores. When the British left, Copley's step-brother Henry Pelham decided it best to leave with them. Susannah's timely decision to leave Boston was wise, for it spared her and her children from what may have been a very unpleasant and very unhealthy sea passage.

It is said that Howe dumped large amounts of military stores into Boston harbor and blew up Castle William with all its stores before his departure. It has been said also that a large amount of military materiel was not destroyed by him, which is puzzling. Left behind were two hundred canons, tons of powder and lead, thousands of muskets, and all sorts of other military stores. Thus, when Washington's regiments left Boston to march on New York, they were reasonably well equipped.

Copley was in Parma, Italy, painting a commissioned copy of the great sixteenth-century Italian painter Correggio's *Saint Jerome* when he was surprised to learn that his family had arrived in London. Their arrival was earlier than he had expected. As soon as he completed the commission, he hurried back to London to be reunited with his wife, son, and two daughters in late fall of 1775. He must have been deeply saddened when told that the health of his second-born son was such that he would not have survived a sea passage, was left in the care of his grandmother, and was expected to live but a short time, as happened. Other sad news for Copley was that the colonies were in a full state of war with Great Britain.

The good news was that Susannah's father, in the aftermath of the Boston Tea Party, had arrived safely in London with some wealth. Copley then availed himself of his father-in-law's generous offer to help him financially. They jointly leased a fine house for ninety-nine years at 21 Leister Square in a prestigious London neighborhood. Sir Joshua lived across the street in a large house that included his studio. James Christie, the well-known auctioneer and founder of Christie's auction house in Pall Mall, lived next door.

The new Copley residence was large enough to accommodate comfortably both a big studio and a growing family that would include two more children, a stay of Henry Pelham for four or five years, and Clarke, who would live with the Copleys for the rest of his life. When Clarke died in 1795, provisions in his will released Copley from a not inconsiderable debt.

CHAPTER 8

What Next

In political terms, Copley's arrival in London was completely unlike that of West's. While they both came from the American colonies, West had arrived about ten years earlier without political baggage. The colonies were still relatively peaceful, and West had been able to establish a relationship of trust with the king without politics being an issue. When Copley arrived in London in 1774, he was weighed down by political baggage. The full-length portrait he had painted of Sam Adams was a powerful one; it showed Adams standing confrontationally before the king's governor demanding that the Massachusetts colony be treated fairly, as stated in its Royal

Charter, and that the British regiments stationed in Boston be withdrawn immediately. A copy of that portrait was commonly printed on broadsheets distributed by radical Sons of Liberty and others throughout the colonies. From the king's point of view, that only could have reflected poorly on Copley. As time passed, the king did come to appreciate Copley's artistry and to praise highly his artistic work, but Copley was never welcomed into royal circles.

When the British evacuated Boston and Henry Pelham went along with them, he took with him not only his own personal papers, but also those Copley had left in his care. Among them was a copy of Copley's 1765 letter to Captain Bruce, wherein he had used the "we" when he described the violence that took place in response to the king's imposition of the Stamp Act. Understandably, the build-up to the American Revolution created concern within the king's security service about the loyalty of some colonialists who had come to England, although as a group, they were generally thought to be Tory. Upon Pelham's arrival in London, he was persuaded to surrender his personal papers to Crown authorities, meaning the king's secret service. When Copley was asked to surrender his papers, he did so, probably believing if he did not they would be seized anyhow. A copy of his letter to Captain Bruce within which he used "we" instead of "they," would have been among those papers conveyed to the king. Consequently, that letter in part may have also influenced the king's subsequent behavior towards him.

Copley's social behavior after settling in London probably intensified the king's unfavorable attitude toward him. Copley and Susannah joined a social group of Bostonians known as the New England Club. They were regular attendees at its weekly dinners until the club turned political and became known as the Brompton Road Tory Club, whose members supported the king's policies towards the colonies. The Copleys discontinued attendance at those dinners, a mistake similar to the one Copley had made in Boston when he had chosen not to identify publicly with either party, Whig or Tory. It was highly likely that Copley's behavior was reported to the king by a member of the club, the king's secret service, or even by West himself when he later came to realize that artistically Copley threatened his need to be first in all things in which he was involved.

Having settled into his new residence with his family, Copley was faced with an urgent need to resume his profession and earn substantial income to support his family. But what should he paint? Large religious scenes were out of the question because West had strengthened his patronage ties with London's powerful Anglican Church leadership and with the king, both of whom favored him exclusively for such work. In London, there were virtually no other sources for significant commissions for religious paintings. Painting historical subjects would take too long to complete and would be too risky financially without a commission, since there was not a market for narrative paintings, and to find a buyer who would pay a fair price was unlikely. Thus, Copley realized that at least for a time he would have to paint portraits. West was happy to see Copley painting portraits and provided him studio space until he could prepare his own. His first painting was a group portrait: *The Copley Family.* He exhibited it at the Royal Academy so as to introduce himself and his family to the London public. While art critics gave it little attention, the public displayed great interest in it. Horace Walpole recorded on his exhibition catalogue: "a painter in it very good," referring to Copley's self-portrait in the painting.

West had about five years earlier begun a painting of his family. It remained unfinished for some time, but was completed in time to be exhibited at the Royal Academy in 1777—the same exhibition that included *The Copley Family.* In West's family painting, he dressed his father and half-brother in Quaker clothing, and himself and his family in stylish clothing, typical of that worn by the Anglican establishment. Thus, he made clear he considered himself Anglican and not Quaker.

CHAPTER 9

A Free Spirit

Almost seventeen years after the birth year of Copley, West, and King George III, Gilbert Stuart was born in a room above his father's snuff mill in Newport, Rhode Island. Like Copley and West, Stuart, while still a youth, aspired to be a painter. At about fifteen years of age, he met Scottish portrait painter Cosmo Alexander, became his apprentice, and was soon accompanying him on his painting tours between Boston and Philadelphia. When Alexander decided to return to Edinburgh, Scotland, Stuart accompanied him. Shortly after their arrival, Alexander died. Although one of Alexander's relatives assisted Stuart for a time,

Stuart soon found himself abandoned, malnourished, and in dire circumstances. Consequently, he worked his way back to America as a common seaman, recovered his health, and set up a portrait practice in Boston. In September 1775, when his parents moved to Nova Scotia, Stuart decided to go to London. At first, life in London was extremely difficult for him. At times he was reduced to near starvation for lack of sufficient income. Even after the Royal Academy accepted four of his portraits for exhibition, his financial situation did not improve until he obtained employment in 1778 as an assistant in West's studio. During his employment there, Stuart found time to paint his own portrait: *Self-Portrait in a Rubens Hat*. When exhibited, it received great public and critical praise. Copley first met Stuart in West's studio.

Stuart's big break as an artist came in 1782. As the story is told, he received a commission to paint his first full-length portrait from a man who greatly enjoyed ice skating, as he did. The day they met to begin the painting, the weather was perfect for skating, so they decided to go skating first. When the portrait, named *The Skater*, was exhibited, it received great praise for its likeness and originality by both the public and the critics. The success of *The Skater* enabled Stuart to leave West's studio and set up his own. Within four years, he had a thriving portrait practice. Such was his popularity that he was said to be greater than any other portrait artist in England except for Sir Joshua, Gainsborough, and Romney. In addition to his thriving portrait practice, Stuart received a commission from the print merchant Boydell to paint fifteen portraits of prominent engravers and artists. This included portraits of Copley and West. Boydell exhibited these portraits between 1783 and 1786 in his studio, placing Stuart's portrait of Copley directly above Copley's grand narrative painting, *The Death of Major Peirson*, also being exhibited. Copley Jr., on seeing his father's portrait, commented that he had never seen such an excellent likeness.

Stuart's clientele consisted primarily of the upper-middle class and some aristocracy. He was highly praised in the press; nonetheless, this extraordinarily gifted colonial portrait painter never received a royal commission.

As Stuart prospered, he began living in high style and in grand residences, in part because portrait painters needed to pay court to their patrons by providing them suitable surroundings while they sat for their portraits. Additionally, studio surroundings had to be such as to convey the aesthetic sensibilities of the artist. Stuart, perhaps because he had been so deprived in his early life, moved to finer and finer residences and filled them with magnificent furnishings, more than what was needed to secure his reputation as a gentleman artist. He entertained lavishly and frequently, and was known to have as many as forty guests at a time. The amount of his debt soon exceeded his ability to service it.

Although his position as a portrait painter was secure in London, learning that he was about to be threatened with debtor's imprisonment for a second time, Stuart fled to Dublin, Ireland, in 1787. He prospered there for five years painting portraits and continued living as lavishly as he had in London. Threatened with a situation similar to that from which he escaped in London, and for some time wanting to paint a portrait of President George Washington, he left Dublin in the spring of 1793 and returned to America, going first to New York City.

Arriving in New York, he was received with great excitement and he painted many portraits there. One was of John Jay, whom he had met in London. Jay was one of the founding fathers of the new nation. He was well known and respected by George Washington, who had chosen Jay to be the first Chief Justice of the Supreme Court. Stuart obtained from Jay a letter of introduction to Washington. Consequently, he went to Philadelphia, then the temporary capital of the new country, and presented his letter of introduction. The president agreed to sit for his portrait. By then, Stuart had obtained about thirty-three commissions for the president's portrait. This suggests that Stuart may have gotten some of these even before he obtained Washington's agreement to sit for his portrait. Stuart was dissatisfied with the results of his first painting of Washington. The president agreed to sit again. It has been suggested that Stuart, by engaging the president in conversation about subjects in which he was interested, got him to relax and enjoy the time he spent sitting for his portrait.

By December 1803, Stuart was painting portraits of notables in Washington, DC, the new capital. Then, in 1805, he permanently settled in Boston. During his lifetime, it is estimated that he had painted some one thousand portraits. His extraordinary ability to capture on canvas a sense of life in his portraits was unequaled among those artists with whom he competed.

Stuart died in 1828, leaving his family in poverty, and he was most likely still addicted to snuff and buying his whisky by the barrel. Shortly before his death, he was asked by the Academy of Florence in Italy to paint a self-portrait for its collection of great artists, one of the highest compliments an artist can receive. He did not get around to doing it. He died truly a free spirit.

CHAPTER 10

Copley Surprises

West was most pleased that Copley decided to paint portraits upon his return from Italy. It was what he expected Copley would do, rather than become his competitor in narrative painting. Besides, West foresaw correctly the strong and growing competition in England among highly talented portrait painters. He recognized the risk to his persona and reputation should his portraiture be compared critically to those by Copley, whose talent was obvious to him; to those by Sir Joshua; to those by the highly talented George Romney, expected to return soon from Italy; and to those painted by the highly successful portrait painter Thomas

Gainsborough, who was expected to move soon to London from Bath. Consequently, West no longer had any interest in seeking commissions for portraiture other than from the royal family, who paid well and gave him status.

To West's great displeasure, Gainsborough became a favorite of the queen and then the king. He found himself displaced by Gainsborough as their favored portrait artist. However, before Gainsborough arrived in London, there is no doubt that painting the royals had been lucrative for West. He had earned from the king some £2,300, a princely sum for portraits of mixed quality.

In 1778, still smarting from Gainsborough gaining favor and patronage from the king and queen, West had to deal with another unwelcomed threat to his artistic standing. Copley received his first major commission to paint a narrative subject. Brook Watson, a prominent London merchant, wanted Copley to paint a dramatic event that occurred in his youth while swimming in the harbor of Havana, Cuba. Watson had been attacked by a shark and lost part of a leg. When *Watson and the Shark* was exhibited at the Royal Academy in 1778, it caused a minor sensation. Copley chose to depict the moment of highest dramatic intensity, the instant just prior to what could be a fatal attack. Viewers had no way of knowing for certain that Watson would be plucked from the jaws of death. Copley's narrative asked the viewer to sympathize with a tragedy, not because it involved a great man or a significant occasion, but because the victim was a human being like the rest of us. The painting received laudatory critical reviews from all three prominent London newspapers.

If West were not by then convinced that Copley would not be content to paint only portraits, what happened next would surely convince him.

It concerned William Pitt, one of Great Britain's great prime ministers. His policies towards France and Spain had led Great Britain to global dominance. In April 1778, a very frail William Pitt, Senior, Earl of Chatham, returned to the House of Lords to debate against a contentious policy concerning independence for the American colonies. There he suffered a stroke, and he died several weeks later. He was arguing strongly against the proposal that all British troops be withdrawn from the colonies. He was arguing for Great Britain to do whatever was necessary to hold America in the British Empire. He saw the colonies as a source of wealth, naval strength, and manpower, as well as a market for English goods.

Copley and West both grasped that Chatham's dramatic and tragic death would be a timely and suitable subject for a narrative painting. Unknown to each other initially, each started painting one without having a commission to do so. Copley saw it as an opportunity to meet some fifty of the most important noblemen in England and possibly to paint individual portraits of some of them. It turned out he received only five commissions. Nonetheless, at least fifty of the fifty-five figures in the painting he painted from life, for Copley always wanted to be as accurate as possible in portraying his subjects. When West learned that Copley was painting the same subject as he, he had to decide either to abandon his effort to paint Chatham's collapse in the House of Lords or complete it. If finished and exhibited, it would surely face public and critical comparison to Copley's work, with an uncertain outcome. On the other hand, not finishing it would suggest to a perceptive public he was concerned about how his artistry might be judged when compared to Copley's. West, who had sharpened his political astuteness by observing the behavior of the nobles at court and the behavior of the men of the two political parties, knew with certainty that some of the lords would be displeased with their positioning in the painting. Thus, on balance it made no sense for him to paint this event. So he did not, but all was not lost. West cunningly, in a grand display of puffery, let it widely be known he was magnanimously stepping aside for the benefit of his colonial colleague.

When the painting was finished, Copley recognized the unlikelihood that a player in the London art market would pay him the £2,000 that he wanted for it. Consequently, he made arrangements to use Christie's auction room in Pall Mall to exhibit it, where viewers would pay to see the painting. When West learned that Copley did not intend to exhibit his painting at the Royal Academy as he expected, Christie was persuaded to renege on his arrangement with Copley. Undeterred, Copley found public exhibition space at the then-defunct Society of Artists. With forethought regarding his fellow artists, who would be exhibiting at the academy, Copley delayed opening his one-painting exhibition to the public until several days after the opening of the Royal Academy's 1779 spring exhibition.

Although critical responses were mixed, *The Death of the Earl of Chatham* was an unqualified public and financial success. In the first six weeks, almost 20,000 people paid to view it. It is said that admission fees grossed more than £5,000. Copley was the first in London to arrange a public display of a single work of art and charge admission to view it. While Copley's success secured his reputation, it did embitter rivals in the Royal Academy. They complained unjustly that he was cravenly driven to make money and should have exhibited his painting at the Royal Academy so the academy would have benefited financially. Hoping then to increase further his income from the painting, Copley sold subscriptions for prints, as was frequently done by artists, including West. He hired an engraver, who promised to complete the plate in four years. Unfortunately, he took ten. After waiting seven years unsuccessfully for someone to buy *The Death of the Earl of Chatham*, Copley finally got the £2,000 he wanted for the painting by raffle.

The great public successes of Copley's *Watson and the Shark* and *The Death of the Earl of Chatham* did not go unnoticed by John Boydell, the principal London printmaker and seller of prints. He wanted another painting, such as West's *The Death of General Wolfe*, from which he could make prints, sell them to the public, and generate substantial profit. However, instead of going back to West, Boydell went to Copley. They considered ten events during the reign of King Charles I and chose his entrance into the House of Parliament with an armed guard to seize those who were plotting to impeach his queen. The title of the painting would be

Charles I Demanding the Five Impeached Members of Parliament.
This was a shrewd choice because this dramatic moment could
be interpreted differently, depending upon the viewer, thereby
having the widest commercial appeal. It could represent to a
viewer that the king should have authority over Parliament, or it
could remind one that Parliament was an independent governing
body, given what happened to Charles I. Copley had already
begun preliminary work on it when a heroic event on an island in
the English Channel prompted Boydell to ask Copley to switch
to another subject, which he did: the death of a Major Francis
Peirson.

Mainly due to the efforts of Benjamin Franklin, the American
ambassador to France, France was providing financial support
to America in its struggle for independence without formally
declaring war against its old enemy England. The Isle of Jersey, an
English possession close off the coast of France,, was so situated
that by 1780 it was a major problem to the allied French and
Americans, it being a base from which privateers were attacking
their ships. The French decided to stop those attacks. On the
night of January 6, 1781, some thousand French troops landed
undetected on the island. The next morning, when the island's
governor awoke in Saint Helier, the capital of the Isle of Jersey,
he found that the French were in complete control of the town.
The French threatened to burn down the town and slaughter its
inhabitants unless the governor ordered all British forces on the
island to surrender. Not knowing what the situation was outside
the capital, the governor was about to issue such an order when

Major Peirson arrived, having assembled a force of some two thousand. He personally and heroically led his men into battle. English victory was achieved after he gave his life in the ensuing combat, being struck by a musket ball in the heart. Thus, Boydell commissioned Copley to paint for £800 what became known as *The Death of Major Peirson*.

CHAPTER 11

King to the Rescue

While all this activity of Copley's was going on, West found himself without commissions from the king, and he began to wonder if he were losing royal favor. West knew the king's courtiers were doing their best to cause this to happen. One was Lord Cathcart, a Scottish baron and cavalry officer, who had distinguished himself during the early years of the American War for Independence. He had returned to London in time to read the news that British forces had succeeded in 1780 in capturing Charleston, South Carolina, having failed in their attempt in 1779.

One morning at court, Lord Cathcart, in a voice calculated to be heard by the king, asked West if he had read the newspapers that morning, to which West replied that he had not. Cathcart told West that His Majesty's troops in South Carolina had gained a splendid victory over the rebels, his countrymen. He continued to needle West by saying that this could not be very pleasant news for him. West recalled that he had replied to Cathcart that certainly it was not pleasant news, for he could never rejoice at the misfortunes of his countrymen. According to West, at this point the king intervened and said to West that his reply to Cathcart did him honor. Then turning to Cathcart, he allegedly told him that in his opinion, any man who is capable of rejoicing in the calamities of his country could never make a good subject of any government. One wonders how West could have remembered such exact detail about this exchange some thirty years later when he dictated this incident to his hired biographer John Galt.

Cathcart's bragging that the Americans were losing the war would be proved wrong within a year, when it became known that General Cornwallis surrendered his army at Yorktown on October 19, 1781, within two days of the fourth anniversary of America's great victory at Saratoga, New York. The war, for all practical purposes, ended then, and the king recognized the independence of the United States of America. It took almost two years of negotiations, however, until formal treaty documents acknowledging America's independence were signed on September 3, 1783.

Lord and Lady Cathcart, as the baron's influence at court increased, worked persistently to stop West from receiving an annual royal stipend of £1,000. Other nobles did so as well, no doubt resentful that a commoner was receiving so much attention from the king. Despite their efforts, West's relationship with the king remained solid until late in his life.

In 1779, the king, perhaps after a discussion with West and Chambers, his architect, decided to make Windsor Castle his chief royal residence. Chambers was charged to modify the castle's architectural style to one more pleasing to the king. West was commissioned to paint religious subjects suitable to adorn two chapels at Windsor, the Royal Chapel in the castle itself and the nearby St. George Chapel. The king assembled a committee of Anglican bishops, who met with West. They chose thirty-six religious subjects that were then approved by the king to be painted. Some of the paintings and cartoon designs for the chapels' stained-glass windows would be very large. The Windsor project would also include paintings of eight historical subjects chosen by the king for display in the castle's reception rooms. For the next ten years, West monopolized all royal artistic patronage connected with the Windsor projects. It involved a vast amount of work. Consequently, he bought a house in Windsor and employed a number of painting assistants, sometimes as many as five, including his two sons from time to time. In addition to payment for his work, West continued to receive a £1,000 annual stipend from the king.

CHAPTER 12

Parting of Ways

*I*n early 1783, the relationship between Copley and West was still socially friendly. Even the wives were getting along well and playing cards together. Being in London had spared both artists from the hardships endured by the American colonists, who had struggled against the king's armies to secure their independence.

Looking back over the almost ten years that had passed since Copley and West met in London, from 1774 to 1783, one may conclude that both artists did quite well professionally and financially. West had become an efficient, commercially minded painter, proudly bragging in a letter to a friend that he was selling his paintings of historical subjects "for prices that no living artist had ever received before." He left unsaid that all his paintings except for a few were painted for the king, who could easily pay exorbitant prices.

During that same period, Copley, in a display of natural genius, painted two grand narratives, *Watson and the Shark* and *The Death of Chatham*, soon to be joined by a third, *The Death of Major Peirson.* He had also gained a reputation as an exceptional portrait painter. He had painted some twenty-three portraits for his clientele, who were military officers, landed gentry, and minor nobility. His fees for portraiture grew to equal those of George Romney, whose fees were second only to those of Sir Joshua. In other words, Copley clearly excelled West in portraiture and was rivaling him in painting historical subjects. Although his future looked bright, the friendly relationship he had with West began to deteriorate rapidly when they went head-to-head in competition to win a major commission.

The Corporation of the City of London wanted a painting to commemorate the British victory over the French and Spanish, who had been blockading the English, who were defending their occupation of Gibraltar. A selection committee visited Copley's studio, where they viewed the completed *The Death of Chatham* and *The Death of Major Peirson,* which was then in the process of being completed. Twelve days later, after a delay requested by West, the committee chose Copley. The contract stated that he would be paid £1,000 for the painting and would be granted rights to exhibit it publicly and publish prints of it. Copley promised to complete the painting within two years. The canvas would be about twenty-five feet by twenty feet.

In 1784, Copley completed and exhibited The *Death of Major Peirson*, again not at the Royal Academy. It was a great success. Critical reviews were full of praise for it. During their private viewing of *The Death of Major Peirson*, the king and queen also expressed great praise for the painting, and it was reported in a newspaper that the king spent nearly three hours examining it.

As a consequence, Copley obtained permission to paint a group portrait of the king's three youngest daughters. Understanding the importance of such an artistic task, Copley promptly set about creating a grand composition of some 104" x 73" that would display the three youngest princesses as real children, not as miniature adults, which was the traditional way to paint royal offspring. It was not only the sheer size of the picture that made it remarkable; it was the originality of the setting within which Copley placed the royal children and how he painted them. He painted the sisters at lighthearted play in a garden full of crisply and finely painted flowers, birds, and dogs. *The Three Youngest Daughters of George III* was finished in time for it to be exhibited at the Royal Academy in 1785.

CHAPTER 13

An Angry Young Man

*I*n 1785, two London newspapers, the popular *Morning Post* and the *Daily Advertiser*, instead of using independent professional critics to provide critical reviews of art as had been their practice, began employing practicing artists instead. This had unfortunate consequences for Copley and West. One of the hired artist critics was John Hoppner. He was believed by some in London to be the son of an attractive lady-in-waiting at court and an unidentified German surgeon who came to England during the reign of King George II. On balance, however, evidence supports the more common belief among Londoners that he was the son of King George III, born prior to his marriage to Queen Charlotte. Hoppner did not deny this until late in life. In his youth, he was removed from the care of his mother by the king, boarded with a Mr. Chamberlain's family, and received a modest weekly allowance from the king. In 1775, he was admitted as a student to the Royal Academy schools. By 1780, he began to exhibit his art there. In 1782, he won the academy's student gold medal for history painting. That same year he made a big mistake: he married Phoebe Wright, the daughter of Patience Wright! Understandably, when the king learned of this marriage, probably from West, who apparently had been instructed by the king to keep an eye on young Hoppner, his anger was such that he cancelled Hoppner's royal allowance. As a result, Hoppner suffered considerable financial difficulty in caring for an extended family that included five children. He blamed West and became spiteful toward him. He transferred his spitefulness to other academicians as well when he was informed that the Royal Academy had rejected his request for membership.

Not surprisingly, Hoppner saw an opportunity to get even with West and other academicians as an anonymous art critic, knowing that what he wrote would have wide circulation in the newspapers. His first critical article in the press pertained to Copley's *The Three Youngest Daughters of George III*. Although his name was not revealed by the newspaper, it became known that it was Hoppner who wrote it. One might have hoped that Hoppner, being an artist, would have seen in the painting its wonderful freshness and inventiveness and reviewed it accordingly, rather than in a mean, scathing way. Regrettably for Copley, other critics followed Hoppner's lead. Understandably, Copley was greatly upset by the negative reviews in the newspapers, and he gave up any hope of gaining portrait commissions from the king and the grand nobility.

Hoppner himself was not spared criticism. Another hired artist critic pointed out in his newspaper article that two poorly painted portraits of elder daughters of King George III by an artist whose name he did not mention unjustly received very high praise from Hoppner. This led the readers to wonder if it were Hoppner who had painted these portraits and was praising himself.

The *Three Youngest Daughters of George III* embodied for the first time one of the most important developments of late eighteenth-century England that pertained to royal children: the recognition of children, even royal children, as individuals with habits and needs different from those of adults. Some two centuries later, this painting would be viewed as glorious. It is remarkable that in 2008, the painting was honored by being included in a catalogue of *The Royal Collection Treasures*. Not one of Benjamin West's paintings are included.

After criticizing Copley, Hoppner turned his attention to West's three paintings on exhibit. His personal attack on West and his paintings in the newspaper was such that they were said to be unprecedented in England and were "felt to be not only cruel but in poor taste." Hoppner suggested that it would have been better if West had been totally unqualified for the arts so that he could have followed some occupation where mind and an intimate acquaintance with human nature were not wanted. That drew

West into personal, nasty exchanges with Hoppner in the press, something he would not do normally because it would show him to be less than the grand gentleman he claimed to be.

Nonetheless, West, still wanting to maintain his persona as a grand gentlemen artist always helpful and generous toward other artists, gave another one of his splendid dinner parties. He invited various members of the artistic community, including the Copleys. He had reason to celebrate. He had received some £1,800 for the four large narrative paintings that had been commissioned by Lord Grosvenor. From the king, he had earned some £2,400 for portraits of royal family members. More recently, the commissions from five years of painting religious subjects at Windsor, along with the royal stipend of £1,000, had provided an average annual income of some £2,000. He enjoyed significant additional income from the sale of prints and other activities. Two more religious paintings were close to being finished. His future looked bright.

CHAPTER 14

A Sneaky Action

For Copley, the year 1785 was tragic. In November, his two children born in London died of infections: Susanna, age nine, and Jonathan, age three. One can imagine how hard it was for the Copley family to cope with this loss and the heartache that ensued, which must have stirred memories of the loss of the newborn in Boston after Susannah departed for London.

In early 1786, the First Lord of the Admiralty, preferring Copley's paintings to those of West, commissioned Copley to paint a replacement for a grand altar painting in the Chapel of the Royal Naval Hospital at Greenwich that had been destroyed by fire. Still filled with heartache over the recent loss of his children, Copley, a devout man at the height of his artistic powers, could have created a magnificent religious painting. One may recall Gavin Hamilton's high praise of Copley's version of *The Ascension* painted in Rome. Copley's ability to paint wonderful religious paintings was also noted by the art critic Horace Walpole. When Walpole visited the academy's new home in Somerset House to view the paintings with which the academicians had adorned it, the only painting to which he applied a descriptive superlative and great praise was Copley's *Samuel Relating to Eli the Judgments of God upon Eli's House.* He recorded: "a most beautiful picture" and went on to praise the painting for how well the biblical story was told. A *Morning Post* critic described it as a masterly picture. This painting, a double portrait, is the dramatic rendering of an Old Testament story of the young boy Samuel hearing the voice of God for the first time. Samuel relates to the priest Eli God's intention to punish Eli's family for the sins of his sons.

Both Copley and West competed for the Greenwich commission. When West learned that not he, but Copley, had been awarded this prestigious commission by the admiralty, he took prompt action that was sneaky and mean. What must have disturbed West and made him extremely anxious was not the commission fee of some £1,300 that Copley would earn. After all, West was fully employed by the king. He had already painted and earned commissions for six of the thirty-six religious subjects approved by the king and the committee of Anglican bishops for the Windsor chapels. In addition, he had begun painting a series of historical subjects chosen by the king to be hung in the reception rooms at Windsor that would earn for him some £7,000.

One wonders why, amid all this painting activity and a guaranteed high level of income, West would risk severely damaging his carefully created persona of being a great and generous gentleman artist by behavior that grossly contradicted it. What explanation is there other than West felt his artistic standing with the king, the court, and the public threatened. Copley had already shown his superiority to West in portrait painting and was a serious rival in painting historical subjects. The Greenwich commission would give Copley the means to challenge West in painting religious subjects. It would afford Copley for the first time an opportunity to paint and display a religious subject on an enormous canvas eighteen feet high to be viewed and commented on by many, including the press. West intuitively knew that Copley could produce a grand religious painting superior to his work. He might even have been haunted by the thought that Copley might get some of the king's patronage for the Windsor project, although it was unlikely. These were risks West was unwilling to take. He always presented himself as the best, as number one, and apparently had a need to see himself that way. In his mind, it was time to rein in Copley!

Contemporaneous newspaper accounts first revealed that West used his influence at court to have the Admiralty's decision overruled and the Greenwich commission given to him. The *Morning Herald* in reporting the change went further and asserted that Copley beyond all comparison was the superior artist. West never denied he had used his influence at court to steal the commission. His silence about the charge suggested to the public he was guilty. Again, his real character pierced the persona he had so diligently and carefully constructed. West completed his painting—*Saint Paul Shaking Off the Viper*—for the admiralty in 1789, for which he received £1,300. As related in the New Testament, it depicts the incident that occurred when Saint Paul was shipwrecked on the Island of Malta.

Nonetheless, during most of the decade of the 1780s, West continued to enjoy the king's patronage. He completed the series of narrative paintings for installation in Windsor, the subjects for which the king had chosen. West also continued to enjoy his special social relationship with the king.

However, by 1789 reservations about the quality of West's painting began to surface more strongly at court. As his canvases got larger and larger, his limitations in draftsmanship to portray well the human form and human emotions became more apparent. One critic commented that West was painting "by the acre" and thereby charging more. By then the queen had become firmly set against him.

Even with the loud whisperings at court about his work, West continued to paint the preapproved religious pictures for Windsor. He may even have prayed every night: "God save the king." West's underhanded behavior destroyed once and for all any remaining good will he and Copley may have shared. Copley never again received a commission for a religious painting.

Boy with Squirrel by John Copley.

The Copley Family by John Copley.

The West Family by Benjamin West.

The Death of General Wolfe by Benjamin West.

The Death of Major Peirson by John Copley.

CHAPTER 15

For Shame, Mr. West

$\mathcal{T}$he year 1787 was not a good year for West. Although his financial future looked bright and would remain so for a decade, he was about to seriously damage his persona by actions that would cause him great public embarrassment. A friendship he had established with French-born art dealer Noel Desenfans became strained over a difference of opinion concerning the alleged authenticity of a painting by the famous seventeenth-century French painter Nicolas Poussin. Benjamin Vandergucht, another art dealer, had shown Desenfans a painting he represented to be a Poussin. To Desenfans, some aspects of the painting appeared not typical of

Poussin, and he told Vandergucht that. Vandergucht responded that West, upon seeing the painting for the first time, had been struck with admiration by its beauty and declared it to be the finest and most exalted Poussin in existence. After obtaining a warranty, Desenfans purchased it for £700. Subsequently, others convinced Desenfans that the painting was not by Poussin, and he sued for return of the purchase price.

Public legal proceedings opened with much attention by the press. Copley, Gainsborough, and West were called to testify. There were two issues before the court: Was the painting a Poussin, and did West tell Vandergucht it was a Poussin? Copley's testimony was simple and straightforward. He refused to say the painting was not a Poussin. He did say he thought it to be an inferior picture. Gainsborough came right to the point. He testified that if he had seen the picture in a shop window, he would not have paid even a paltry sum for it. Cross examination of Gainsborough brought some humor into the courtroom when Vandergucht's counsel asked him what he meant when he used the phrase "the painter's eye." Gainsborough replied that the painter's eye was to him what the lawyer's tongue was to the counselor.

Finally, West was called to testify, and he waffled on the first issue. While looking at the picture in question, he had it turned one way and then another, over and over again, while saying some aspects of it were like Poussin, but others were not. On the second issue, West admitted that he might have said some flattering things about the picture to Vandergucht. Then, searching for an excuse, he said nonsensically that was because he was of the habit of not condemning that which he could not applaud. The verdict was for Desenfans, who got his money back. West was severely ridiculed in the press. With the passage of time, the broken friendship between Desenfans and West seemed to be mended.

With the assistance of Francis Bourgeois, a young man whom the Desenfans family had welcomed into their home, Desenfans succeeded in becoming a wealthy art dealer. Bourgois and Desenfans assembled a large collection of fine paintings that by happenstance were linked to the catastrophe that enveloped Poland in the eighteenth-century. Much of the art Desenfans had collected was purchased for King Stanisław Augustus II of Poland, who chose Desenfans to be his exclusive agent for acquiring in England and France great art for what was intended to be the national art collection of Poland. The Polish king was so pleased with Desenfans that he honored him by appointing Desenfans his Consul General in London and knighted Bourgeois in gratitude for the services he had provided. Thereafter, Bourgeois was recognized in England as Sir Francis.

Disastrous historical events prevented Poland's King Stanislaw from following through with his plans. When Austria, Prussia, and Russia seized large parts of Poland in 1793, Desenfans had already acquired a large number of paintings for King Stanislaw. But the king now lacked the funds to pay for them. Two years later, the rest of Poland was seized by Russia. King Stanislaw was forced to abdicate and was placed in perpetual house arrest by Catherine the Great of Russia.

Left with a sizeable collection of fine paintings that had been chosen for a Polish royal collection, Desenfans sought a permanent home for them. He approached the new Tsar of Russia and the British Government, among others, but to no avail. Being an insatiable buyer and collector, he increased his inventory of paintings considerably. From his entire holdings, he chose the very best to be exhibited in his large residence. At that point, he and Sir Francis pledged that the Desenfans collection would always remain intact and none of the paintings ever sold. Thus, an eventual permanent home for the collection was needed. In pursuit of this goal, Desenfans prepared a catalogue of his collection and went to West for comment on its preface. Apparently, West did not want to provide comment and instead recommended that Reverend Bromley be employed by Desenfans to work on the catalogue. What Desenfans got from Bromley was a preface that made West the great man of the arts. Desenfans concluded that unless there was something in it for him, meaning West, one generally should not expect anything from him.

Desenfans died in 1807 and willed the collection to Sir Francis, who upon his death in 1811 bequeathed the collection of over 350 paintings to Dulwich College near London, with stipulations that the collection would always remain intact and open to the public to view. It included over fifty-six paintings that were originally intended for Poland. A grant of £10,000 came with the collection, of which £2,000 was used to construct a gallery building designed by the great architect Sir John Soane. Now called the Dulwich

Picture Gallery, this was England's first public art gallery, opening its doors in 1817. It was a great gift indeed that Desenfans and Bourgeois bequeathed to the English people.

For some years West had been representing himself as an art connoisseur competent to correctly identify and assign value to Old Master paintings, but he was not. His actions regarding the Walpole collection incensed the English people and caused him shame. He boasted that he had arranged the sale of the Robert Walpole collection of some 174 old master paintings to the Empress Catherine the Great of Russia and bragged that he got £40,555, the price he set for it. Robert Walpole was one of England's great prime ministers, extremely wealthy, and the father of Horace Walpole. The Walpole collection was reputed to be the finest and most famous private art collection in England and among the finest in the world. Empress Catherine the Great of Russia, who was an immensely wealthy, voracious collector of great art, was willing to pay large sums for entire collections and wanted this one. She also knew how to drive a hard bargain. After two months of negotiations with Mr. West, it is said she paid only about £36,000 for the Walpole collection, and not the price West bragged he got. This sale outraged the English people, who saw in it the loss of a whole chapter of British history and culture.

In 1787, Copley was hard at work on the Gibraltar commission that he had been awarded by the Corporation of the City of London. His painting *The Siege of Gibraltar* was progressing well when several senior German officers from Hanover who had led mercenary regiments at Gibraltar for the British raised objections to the painting's composition. They were displeased with their positioning on the canvas, which they insisted did not show well enough their actual involvement in the struggle. They demanded the composition be altered so it would show them as they wanted. They also insisted on being painted life-size instead of half-size, although half-size was what had been agreed upon between Copley and the Corporation of the City of London. These and other considerations required major changes to the painting's composition.

The Corporation of the City of London agreed that Copley would travel to Hanover to paint the portraits of these officers so they could be included in the painting as life-sized figures and be clearly recognizable. This necessitated a reworking of the entire composition and approximately doubling its size. These new requirements, of course, would significantly lengthen the time Copley would need to complete the painting.

Apparently still smarting from Copley's competitive victory over him by winning the Gibraltar commission and finding out the painting would take much longer to complete, West schemed against Copley. With malicious intent, West suggested to John Trumbull, an independent American artist working out of his studios, that he consider quickly painting something from the Gibraltar struggle. His suggestion, to which Trumbull agreed, was aimed at bringing a good painting to market before Copley could finish his grander treatment of the event and thereby diminish the market's interest in Copley's work when it was finally completed.

By the spring of 1791, Copley's *The Siege of Gibraltar* was completed. It had taken him four years. He exhibited it under a grand tent in Green Garden. Although a large number of people flocked to see the painting, Copley estimated about 60,000, it received only scant attention by the press, which must have been a great disappointment to Copley. When Copley asked to be paid an additional amount for having to produce a painting twice the size of that originally proposed, with figures life-size rather than half-size, he was paid in May 1793 only the £500 still due him under the original contract. It was not until six years later, in 1799, that the issue concerning payment for the Gibraltar painting was settled. By then, Copley, being under severe financial stress, accepted the offered amount of £100.

Still trying to be justly compensated for the magnitude of his effort, Copley turned to the print market, but the publication of the engraving of the painting was unsuccessful. As anticipated by West, the public had lost interest in an event that occurred many years earlier. Having expended so much effort on this project when Copley was at the peak of his creative powers, this was a sad conclusion. The sweet taste of victory in winning the commission from Benjamin West yielded to bitterness. The behavior of the Corporation of the City of London was shameful.

CHAPTER 16

A Coronation

During the first thirteen years of the Royal Academy, its affairs progressed smoothly under the leadership of its first president Sir Joshua Reynolds. Following the death of Sir Joshua in 1792, West, known to be a favorite of the king, easily won election to the presidency, since the academicians knew without the king's approval no one could occupy that office. In his inaugural address, West announced to the academicians that "not on my part, but to do honor to the office to which you have so kindly elected me, when sitting in this chair I shall presume in the future to wear my hat in this Assembly." Despite his disclaimer, one might detect a hint of self-coronation.

The extent of his self-admiration became apparent when, having been offered a knighthood by the king, he declined it, remarking that anything less than baronetcy was inappropriate for someone such as himself.

Copley refused to accept West's triumph gracefully, in light of his behavior toward him since 1785. Not surprisingly, sharp conflict arose almost immediately between these two artists on academy matters. West and his leadership group consistently rejected ideas and suggestions put forth by Copley. The first big quarrel erupted in the assembly the year after West's ascension to his throne-like chair. Of all things that could have sparked it, it was a book. Copley discovered in the academy's library the first of a two-volume work titled *A Philosophy and Critical History of the Fine Arts* written by the Reverend Robert Anthony Bromley, who was just a few years older than West. West and Bromley knew each other well. The West family regularly attended religious services at Fitzroy Chapel, founded by Reverend Bromley and where he was the Minister. The chapel was not far from the Wests' residence, where the Bromley's were frequently received socially by the Wests. West had painted their individual portraits and donated two religious paintings to Fitzroy Chapel. It was generally believed that Bromley helped West write the discourses he as president was expected to deliver annually at the Royal Academy.

Their relationship was such that it was almost certain West would have made suggestions on the content of Bromley's book. It praised him and no other academician. It declared that West's *The*

Death of General Wolfe was a great modern example of narrative history painting. It completely ignored Copley's narrative paintings, which were so highly praised. Copley was outraged. It gave him good reason to attack West. At the beginning of an assembly meeting, with West in the chair, Copley rose and declared the book unfit for the holdings of the academy and moved to condemn and expel it from the academy's library. His motion was quickly seconded. Then, after two hours of tedious discussion, it was decided to postpone voting until those who had not read the book would have time to do so.

West realized that if Copley's motion were to be carried in the assembly, the public would soon know about it. Most probably, those who could afford to purchase the book would ignore it and sales would plummet. West responded to that threat by declaring that the book was the property of the king and therefore should not be turned out of the academy library. This was nonsense. The academy had long since become financially independent, and if the king had directed it be purchased, West would surely have brought forward that fact. He had not.

West could not prevent the outcry within the Royal Academy from reaching the public. The academicians, who were unfairly treated in Bromley's book, made public their displeasure with reasonable restraint. Reverend Bromley in turn responded with a series of outrageous, nasty, and sometimes vulgar letters addressed to them and had them published in the press. As a friend of Bromley, one would expect West would have tried to calm him down and soften the attacks. If he tried, he failed. One would also expect that as president of the Royal Academy, West would have spoken out on behalf of his fellow academicians. He did not. One wonders, could it be that West partnered with Bromley in the book's authorship and publication, and perhaps even provided the money to publish it? Although West was urged by several academicians to end his relationship with Bromley, he did not. Was there a bit of subtle blackmail in the relationship? Although the assembly did not bring Copley's motion to a vote, almost the entire assembly membership seemed to disapprove of the book. When Volume II was published in 1795, it did not sell, and the assembly voted seventeen to four with five abstaining to cancel its subscription—one of the five being West.

Ten years later, West would lose his spiritual adviser and like-minded friend. In the winter, Bromley fell into a puddle of cold water, where he sat for a time in wet clothes. Two days later he died of brain fever. At the end of his life, the Reverend Bromley was found to be immoral, having seduced a young girl who sang in his chapel and died by neglect in childbirth.

CHAPTER 17

A Scam

In 1795, the same year that the Royal Academy Assembly voted against purchasing the second volume of Bromley's book, West began an ill-advised relationship with a stranger. He was Thomas Provis, who called on him seeking advice about an astounding discovery. He claimed he had found in Italy, in an old chest of his sea captain grandfather, a copy of a valuable manuscript on painting. Although he was not a painter, he said his attractive twenty-year-old daughter, Ann Jemima, was an aspiring one. She thought the document of her great-grandfather described materials and techniques used by Venetian artists of the sixteenth-century to create wonderfully rich and luminous colors in their paintings—sometimes referred to as the Venetian secret. Numerous artists over the centuries had tried to replicate the Venetian secret, but all had failed.

According to Provis, using the old copy as a guide, Ann Jemima applied herself toward imitating the Venetian painters, but a fire in their residence had destroyed the copy. Nevertheless, he said that his daughter had learned much from it. He then showed West some examples of what she had painted. This led to the declared purpose of his visit. Since Ann Jemima was of delicate constitution and, as her father, he was concerned about his ability to provide for her welfare, he wondered if she were to share her work on the Venetian secret with West, could this produce some financial benefit to her?

West studied the samples and apparently thought they did show some evidence of the Venetian secret. He recalled that while in Italy in the early 1760s, while copying Titian's *Venus of Urbino*, he had tried to produce the same effect in the use of color as the Venetian painters had but was unsuccessful. The possibility of new information about the technique was irresistibly intriguing to West. He suggested to Provis that with Ann Jemima's help in remembering what was in the manuscript, he would make an experimental painting. It was agreed that the work would be done in the Provis residence, so there would be no interruptions.

When West went there to do the painting, he went alone. The painting turned out badly. It was then agreed that Provis would prepare canvases differently and that West, with Ann Jemima's help, would try again. According to West, although this agreement had been reached, he had tried to call on them a number of times over the months, but each time they were not at home. Finally, in October 1796, West reconnected with Provis. At the Provis residence, with the assistance of Ann Jemima, he produced a second experimental painting. This time West became excited about the results. As yet, West had told no one at the academy about his activities. He was about to be duped, as other academicians would be.

Although West and Provis had agreed that Ann Jemima would receive financial benefit for what she had been doing with West, so far she had received none. Provis then approached several academicians, told them about West's activities, and complained that he thought West intended to steal the Venetian secret to his sole advantage and pay Ann Jemima nothing. Provis then suggested that the academy might want to buy into what West was trying to keep to himself, or academicians individually could purchase instruction from Ann Jemima with license to use it. The news about West's behavior circulated among the academicians and damaged his standing with them. At least eight academicians accepted Provis' offer. Copley was not one of them. Then the young lady, with her alleged knowledge of the Venetian secret and delicate constitution, went from academician to academician explaining what she knew. She collected from each one £10.

Meanwhile West, using one of the canvases that had been prepared by Provis in the so-called manner of the Venetians, was making progress on a painting he titled *Cicero Discovering the Tomb of Archimedes*, which he wanted to complete in time for exhibition at the academy in April 1797, thereby showing himself to be the first to master the Venetian secret. Not yet sure of how it would work when painting human figures, he used a mixed manner of painting. He painted the figures in his normal way, but painted the background scene in the manner of the Venetians, to the extent he understood it. While the painting looked fine when it left West's studio, it did not remain that way. While on exhibition, the scene began to darken with the passage of time and transformed itself from a daylight discovery by Cicero, as intended, to a moonlit one. West was greatly embarrassed. When the fraud was finally exposed, attacks in the press and by satirists were far worse for West than for the other academicians. All had been conned, but since West, as president of the Royal Academy, should have known better and behaved differently, the attacks on him were merciless. The persona that West had created for himself was continuing to erode. Provis and his daughter of delicate constitution disappeared without a trace.

CHAPTER 18

Too Many Wives

One may recall that Copley had started work on a commission from John Boydell, the principal London printmaker and seller of prints, to paint the event in English history when King Charles I confronted Parliament, but he agreed to stop working on it when Boydell requested that he paint instead another subject, the heroic death of a Major Francis Peirson. When that painting was completed in 1784, Copley returned to the task of finishing *Charles I Demanding*. With the help of historians, he identified fifty-six individuals who were believed to have been in the parliament in 1642 when the king entered it in pursuit of those intending to impeach his queen.

To depict these men as accurately as possible, Copley spent an entire summer traveling about England copying images of them from portraits, prints, miniatures, medallions, and even from a death mask. He was granted special permission to gain access to a portrait of the king painted by the famous Flemish portrait painter Anthony Van Dyke, court painter to King Charles I.

Having gathered and copied all the images he could, Copley took another step. He adjusted the appearances of the images to take into account any changes that time most likely etched on them. This extra attention to detail reflected Copley's strong conviction that an artist of historical narrative should be as accurate as possible. He believed such accuracy would enhance interest in the painting, stimulate greater appreciation for it, increase its value, and thereby bring in good financial return for the time and effort he expended. This was Copley's theory, and it was what drove him to such extraordinary efforts for historical accuracy. But, sadly, the painting of Charles I did none of that for him.

Weighted down by debt and not having started a new narrative painting for over fifteen years, Copley decided to do so again. He had painted a sketch of Lord Duncan, a well known British Admiral, Commander and Chief of the British fleet in the North Sea. It may have been in conversation with the admiral that Copley conceived the idea of a painting that would reestablish his primacy in narrative painting and there by improve his financial situation.

The subject for the new narrative depicts the dramatic moment when Admiral de Winter, commander of the Dutch fleet, presents his sword in surrender to Admiral Lord Duncan. Lord Duncan gallantly declined to take it, displaying respect for the heroic performance of the Dutch. The Dutch had reluctantly allied themselves with the French in order to retain their independence from France by denying the British access to the North Sea. *The Victory of Lord Duncan* is considered one of Copley's finest narrative paintings.

In May 1799, Copley exhibited *The Victory of Lord Duncan* in a tent along with his finally finished *Charles I Demanding* and the re-exhibition of *The Death of Lord Chatham*. Critical reviews of these paintings were very favorable, but the London public in general did not turn out to view them. By the turn of the century, public interest had largely turned away from narrative painting to that of landscape. Copley tried to get London's Court of Common Council to purchase *Charles I Demanding*, but failed. All was not lost, however. In early 1802, Duncan's aunt purchased for some £1,000 the grand narrative painting of the impressive victory her nephew had won.

Still in need of funds, and after a long time wrangling about the value of his Beacon Hill property, Copley finally settled the issue for £4,200. In his view, this amount was less than the property's value. As his son had advised him, considering the complications of land ownership that existed after the American Revolution, it was all that he was assured to get. That settlement, along with proceeds from the sale of two hundred prints of *The Death of Chatham* and income from painting a number of excellent portraits, Copley's financial situation improved for a time, and he barely avoided foreclosure on the Copley residence. It was then that he gave serious thought to returning to America, but because Susannah was reluctant to do so, they did not.

In 1800, prospects for greater financial well-being increased for Copley. He received from Sir Edward Knatchbull, a wealthy English widower, a commission to paint a very large family portrait. The painting was to include himself, his twelve children, and hunting dogs, on a canvas about twelve feet high by eighteen feet wide. All the figures were to be life size. Sir Edward's first wife had died in 1784, his second in 1799. In August of 1800, Sir Edward took Copley to his mansion in Marsha. Copley remained there for most of September and October working on picture design and sketching individual portraits, after which he returned to London and started to work on the painting itself. Then, Sir Edward surprised Copley by asking him to include his deceased first and second wives in the painting. Copley determined that the best way to put their images in the painting, with minimal disturbance to its general design, would be to place them among the clouds. That appears to have been acceptable to Sir Edward—until the next surprise. Along comes wife number three, and how will she be fitted into the design? Then later on, where shall the new baby go, and finally, what to do with images of wife one and wife two, whom apparently wife number three did not want in the painting?

At this point, Copley had had enough. He finished the painting, leaving the two deceased wives among the clouds. He informed Sir Edward of his intent to exhibit the painting at the Royal Academy's summer exhibition and requested his approval. Although he received no response from Sir Edward, he started preparations to move the huge painting from his studio to the academy's exhibition hall. When West heard that the council had approved a request from Copley for a little more time before he had to deliver his huge painting *The Knatchbull Family* for exhibition, he urged council members to withdrawal their approval. They refused.

The painting finally being completed, Copley billed Sir Edward £600 more than what was originally agreed. Sir Edward refused to pay the extra charge. The matter went to arbitration, which began in March 1804. West, assisted by several other academicians, spoke on behalf of Sir Edward. West said that he thought the £1,200 initially agreed upon was still a very handsome price for the painting. He said that he had been paid that same amount for a painting about the same size. However, West failed to point out that the painting about which he spoke had been painted some eighteen years earlier. To be fairly compared, West should has taken into account the some 80 percent inflation that had occurred during those eighteen years. He did not. Besides, Copley's design was more complex and became more so as changes were made, as ordered by Sir Edward. West's testimony appeared to be that of an artist who knew better, but with willful intent was set upon frustrating Copley's effort to be paid a fair price. Hoppner, apparently still harboring a dislike for Copley, also spoke against him, saying that the price Copley wanted was too high.

Copley Jr., only being several months away from being called to the legal bar, had all the skills of a barrister, one who could argue before English courts, and represented his father. He mustered nine artists, including five academicians, who spoke in favor of Copley's demand for £1,800. Their testimony asserted that painting the landscape background involved more work and was more difficult than simply painting backgrounds of fourteen separate full-length portraits. This was very significant testimony. Copley Jr. then argued that the changes to the picture's design demanded by Sir Richard and wife number three justified Copley's reasonable demand for an additional payment of £600. Results of the arbitration were not made public, most likely as a condition of settlement, perhaps to permit Sir Edward to save face. That and young Copley's argumentation suggests the outcome favored his father. Subsequently, Copley and Susannah were invited by Sir Edward to the Knatchbull residence, where they were well received. While there, Copley assured the family painting was well hung.

Young Copley's admission to the legal bar in 1804 and his apparent successful representation of his father in the arbitration may not have occurred if a family event in 1800 had not. Obtaining admission to the legal bar in England was a long, costly, and arduous process. Copley's financial situation was such that he could not help his son, although he certainly wanted to do that. But his new son-in-law Gardiner Greene, a wealthy Bostonian widower whom his daughter Elizabeth had married, responded to Copley's request to provide some £1,000 needed by Copley Jr. to complete the process of becoming a barrister. At the same time, however, within the family there was a hint of bad news. In a letter to her daughter, now Mrs. Elizabeth Greene, Susannah wrote that Copley Sr. had experienced an ill turn, but then he recovered. He had been seized by numbness in his hand, which likewise affected his legs and feet, that lasted but a short time.

CHAPTER 19

Loss of Royal Favor

In March of 1802, the Treaty of Amiens between France and Great Britain established an armistice that lasted about a year. This short peace would end when Napoleon Bonaparte, fortified by funds from his sale to America of the Louisiana Territory, a huge swath of land west of the Mississippi River, made demands on the English that he knew would be unacceptable. And he began maneuvers that led to his occupation of Hanover, ruled by George III. The very real threat of invasion loomed over England. Only Russia and England stood in Napoleon's way to complete his conquest of Europe.

At the Royal Academy, West, as president, continued to enjoy a solid majority in both the assembly and the council, and came to see himself as the senior executive officer of that institution, displaying yet again an inflated sense of self. However, some academicians, displeased with West's conduct in regard to the Bromley and Provis incidents, withdrew their support and formed in November of 1800 the Academy First Club. It was a place where academicians who disagreed with the agendas formulated by West's supporters could caucus in opposition. Copley, sometimes assisted by James Wyatt, a friend and fellow academician, led the minority group. Wyatt was a highly skilled architect and popular in eighteenth-century England. After Chambers retired, Wyatt became the king's surveyor-general and did much to assist in George III's effort to restore St. George's Chapel at Windsor. At court, he was a favorite, particularly of the queen.

The constant squabbling within the academy displeased the king, who became annoyed with both West and Copley. His annoyance worried West, who from the 1790s had cause to be a nervous courtier. And yet, West was about to make matters worse for himself with the king. It turned out that it was not his stay in Paris itself that would diminish even more his standing with the king, but rather his actions while there.

A number of academicians, but not Copley, eager to take advantage of the cessation of hostilities with France, went to Paris to view French art collections and those plundered by Napoleon's armies. West also wanted to go to Paris but thought it advisable first to seek permission from the king, and so he did. Not receiving an answer, he went anyway. West departed London on August 27, 1802.

His declared purpose was to reach an agreement with French Academy officials that any artist recommended to them by the President of the Royal Academy would be given all the advantages granted to French artists for the purpose of study. West might also have been curious about the possibilities of employment in Paris.

When West went to Paris, he took his small painting, *Death on the Pale Horse*, which he intended to exhibit in the French Academy exhibition of modern artists scheduled to open at the Louvre in early September. He was hospitably received and invited to choose the place where he wished it to be hung. One day, learning that Napoleon would visit the French Academy exhibition, West rushed to the Louvre and positioned himself so that he stood close to his painting. When Napoleon stopped to view it, West was able to exchange a few amiable words with him.

Just before returning to London on October 10, 1802, West behaved in such a way that it appeared he no longer cared what King George III might think of him. He lavishly entertained a large group of people, among whom were a number of well-known British anti-monarchists, one being the notorious Irish terrorist Arthur O'Connor.

Upon West's return to London, a major dispute erupted in the academy for which he was totally responsible. A constitutional issue arose that put the two factions—those supporting West and those supporting Copley—into conflict with each other. The disagreement regarded the relative powers between the assembly and the council. West had come to see himself as the senior executive officer of the academy, with full powers over both the assembly and the council. He was about to learn that he was not.

When it was Copley's turn to serve on the council, the composition of the council was such that West lost his majority control of it. In a display of pique, West ignored the council and its prerogatives, as stated in the founding documents. Instead he used his control of assembly meetings to appoint special committees of academicians that would approve and carry out what he wanted done.

In early 1803, the council responded to West's actions by sending a letter to him. It requested that he, along with proper officers of the academy, carry forward to the king a request to know what his view might be as to whether the assembly had the power to appoint committees to perform any part of the duties or business of the council. West was told that if he should not do it, other means would be found to get it done.

West ignored the council's request. Instead, he organized an assembly meeting with a slim quorum of ten out of a body of forty academicians, who then voted to suspend from the academy council Copley, Wyatt, and three others opposed to him. These academicians then appealed to the king for redress. The king settled the matter in favor of West's opposition. When West presented his case, the king told him that Copley's opposition party had gotten to him first by a day, and he had ordered that members who had been suspended be reinstated and the academy's records concerning the dispute and all minutes relating to their suspension be expunged from the academy's proceedings. He told West that what he had done was wrong. The authority of the council, in respect to administration of academy affairs, was confirmed supreme over the assembly. Also, the king reminded West that only the council had authority to expend funds, not the assembly, nor the president. Thus, West experienced a royal dressing down.

Late in 1803, if West needed additional confirmation that he had lost the king's favor, he got it when he tried to call on the king at Windsor and was told that he was not to come there.

Two years later, things grew even worse for West. It was Copley's turn to serve on the hanging committee. This committee of academicians decided what paintings would be accepted for annual exhibitions and where on the walls of the academy they would be hung. Copley noticed that a religious picture that West wanted to exhibit appeared to be one that West had exhibited at the academy in 1776. Even after almost three decades, that exhibition was still memorable to Copley, it being the first time he had viewed a Royal Academy exhibition. To be sure, Copley checked the academy records. They confirmed that in 1776 West had indeed exhibited a painting of the same religious subject, *Hagar and Ishmael in the Wilderness*. Exhibiting a painting more than once in the academy would break a fundamental academy rule.

Copley reported to council members what he had discovered. They checked the records for what had been exhibited in 1776 and confirmed that Copley was correct. In careful examination of the painting, a failed attempt to remove its dating of 1776 was noted. Council members were shocked by West's behavior. They met without West present and rejected the painting.

Leaks to the press produced in West a display of extreme self-righteous rage. He first learned about the council's action from a newspaper. He then claimed that the painting was not the one exhibited in 1776. He said that he had sold that painting after its exhibition and then after re-acquiring it in 1802 made alterations to such an extent that it was no longer the same painting. Neither the press nor the public believed any of that. What publicly hurt West the most was that the *Morning Post* reported the fact that academicians, after careful examination of the painting, found a failed attempt to remove the date 1776 from it. One wonders why West chose not to disclose what he had done to the painting before he presented it to the hanging committee. In a last attempt, West failed to prevent the painting's removal from the exhibition by claiming such action would prevent timely publication of the exhibition catalogue.

Not surprisingly, by 1804, many stories were circulating about the king's dislike of West. William Beechey was thought by many to be the source of these stories. He had become the artist most favored at court and had painted his grand *George III and the Prince of Wales Reviewing Troops*. It was extremely well received, especially by the queen. Consequently, he became the only artist after Sir Joshua to be knighted by King George III. Sir William's dislike, or perhaps hatred, of West is understandable, given Sir William's charge that West had told the king that he and his wife were not married. If true, she would be seen as an improper person to be received by the queen. Sir William settled the issue by producing the marriage certificate. Again, it seems probable that West was attacking an artist whom he saw as a threat to his standing within the artistic community. West, as was his practice when accused of wrongdoing, did not respond to Sir William's charge. One wonders if there were ever a time when West expressed mea culpa.

Chapter 20

West Has Problems

With the beginning of the new century in 1800, one might expect that West would have engaged in some retrospection and reviewed his financial situation and prospects. If he did, he would recall that he had long been accustomed to living extremely well, but that was changing. The ongoing war with France had reduced his income from print sales to only 10 percent of the annual £500 he had been making from those sales. Heightened inflation and imposition for the first time of an income tax had increased his expenses to a point where they were exceeding his annual income by some £600, even after he reduced his servants from six to three, and though he was still getting the £1,000 royal stipend. The king had not yet paid him £15,000 still owed for his work at Windsor.

West's economic prospects became catastrophic when Wyatt, as instructed by the queen (the king being disabled) told him to stop all work at Windsor. The queen for some years had shown a strong dislike of West, and in November of 1800 concluded it would be a waste to spend any more money for the work coming out of his studios. The king being incapacitated, she then even went so far as attempting to stop payments of the royal stipend the king had been providing West. But the manager of the privy purse told the queen that it could not be done without the king's order to do so. When the king recovered, he did pay West the £15,000 due him, but there would be no more royal commissions.

As West's luck would have it, he found a new patron, William Beckford, whose father had accumulated a huge fortune in land in the West Indies tied to the sugar trade. At age ten, William inherited his father's fortune. Soon after their meeting, West received from him a £1,000 annual stipend for two or three years and commissions to paint a number of portraits and narrative pictures. Beckford eventually came to own eighteen paintings by West, some of which may not have been purchased directly from him. As with West's other work, there were issues regarding quality. One was bluntly described in 1838 by a French lady visitor to the Beckford mansion. After viewing West's portrait of Beckford's mother, Maria Hamilton Beckford, this French lady concluded that "West certainly knew nothing of portrait painting" and referred to the entire composition "as dry and hard, as if painted by a Chinese novice."

Although the grand Beckford residence was some eighty-five miles from London and required two days of travel to get there, West at first went there frequently. Having lost the king's patronage, it was vital to West that Beckford's patronage be cultivated; however, there was a major problem. As West must have known, Beckford had become a social pariah.

After being married only a little over a year, Beckford was apprehended in what appeared to be a homosexual act with a sixteen-year-old boy. In England, sodomy was a capital crime. Beckford fled England with his wife and their infant daughter. Their two-year marriage ended in Switzerland when his twenty-four-year-old wife died in childbirth. His two daughters were taken from him, and he never remarried. Beckford was generally thought to be bisexual.

West's persistence in keeping Beckford's patronage may have contributed to some loss of support for West in the academy. In 1802, his presidency of the academy was challenged for the first time, although unsuccessfully, by Wyatt, who was then a favorite of both the king and queen.

West received another blow when the king and queen again ignored him at Windsor. When the time approached for the 1804 presidential election, West, unsure of what the election outcome would be, resigned from his post as academy president. Wyatt was elected. West, stung by events, adopted an attitude of I'll show you—and so he did. Being free from work for the king and duties at the Royal Academy, he had time to complete a painting he had started that was based on a recent, great event.

On the twenty-first of October, 1805, off the southwest coast of Spain near the Cape of Trafalgar, a great naval battle was fought between a British fleet of twenty-seven ships of the line and a combined French and Spanish fleet of thirty-three ships of the line. The British fleet was commanded by Lord Horatio Nelson, already famous in Britain for his victories at sea. His leadership and tactical employment of the British fleet at Trafalgar produced one of Britain's greatest naval victories. That was the defeat of the Franco-Spanish fleet, which lost twenty-two ships; the British lost none. With a great victory already assured, Nelson tragically fell victim to a sniper in the rigging of an enemy ship and died. When the news reached London, West and Copley both recognized there was a high probability that a painting of this stunning event would be a great success with the public. Each quickly started to paint Nelson's victory. Fortunately for West, Copley fell and injured his painting arm such that he could not return to painting soon enough to compete. Then to show spiteful disdain for the Royal Academy, West opened a public exhibition at his residence on the same day that the Royal Academy opened its annual exhibition. Publically, his painting was a great success; about 30,000 people, according to West, were believed to have viewed it. The admission charge and sale of prints made from the painting brought in large sums. West's conduct was worse than that of which he and Chambers had accused Copley when he had exhibited his *The Death of Chatham* in 1781. Copley, at least, had waited until several days after the Royal Academy's opening of its annual exhibition.

In the meantime, Wyatt having proved to be an incompetent Royal Academy president, lost the king's approval and resigned. A majority of academicians, with the king's approval, persuaded West to resume the presidency. He did.

CHAPTER 21

The Elgin Marbles

The Scottish nobleman Thomas Bruce, seventh Earl of Elgin, who served as British Ambassador to the Ottoman Empire from 1799 to 1803, took from the Parthenon and other structures on the Acropolis in Athens, Greece, a large number of marble sculptures and shipped them to London. Although the Parthenon, the temple to Athena, had fallen to ruin with only its outer shell standing, Elgin helped himself not only to fragments lying about, but also had his workmen remove sculptures from the Parthenon itself and from other buildings on the Acropolis. What Elgin did was lauded by many, who saw in his actions a means to preserve priceless objects from antiquity at huge cost to himself; but many were opposed who thought Elgin had stolen from the Greeks a huge and irreplaceable part of their ancient cultural heritage. At first, West joined the latter group.

It was not until June, 1807, that Elgin invited a few connoisseurs and artists to view part of what had been shipped to England from Greece. He had the sculptures and fragments installed in a large shed, there to be joined by other shipments. These sculptures became known as the Elgin Marbles. One of the artists to view the sculptures was Benjamin Robert Hayden, a serious scholar and a greatly talented art student in the academy schools to whom Elgin granted daily permission to study and sketch the marbles. These marble sculptures included depictions of gods, men, and monsters. In every detail, they were sculpted with amazing realism and were thought to be the highest expression of ancient Greek artistic genius. They dated from the fifth century BC.

Hayden was fascinated by the Elgin Marbles, not only because of his deep interest in the study of anatomy as the underpinning of convincing naturalism, but also because he believed the marbles provided evidence that ancient Greek artists had also studied anatomy seriously, for the Greeks were the first to represent humans, gods, and animals as though they were living beings and not just static images.

Hayden had been working twelve-hour-long days over a number of months studying and sketching the marbles before West arrived on the scene in the winter of 1807–1808. West was then sixty-nine years old. He was surprised to find Hayden there hard at work. This encounter afforded the elderly West a wonderful opportunity to behave in a truly generous way by not competing with Hayden, but rather by providing encouragement to a highly talented young artist more than two generations younger than he. Instead, as he had done over and over again in a long life, West strove to put himself first. Since he could not claim to be the first to have studied and sketched the marbles, he tried another way to get his name permanently associated with them.

West spent three weeks hurriedly studying and drawing sketches of the marbles. When Haydon saw the sketches, he concluded that West had learned nothing from them; this from an artist who was a serious student of anatomy. It is said that West then hurriedly painted six large compositions, which have not been found, in which he claimed to have incorporated artistic values from antiquity that he had observed in the Elgin Marbles. In February of 1809, West wrote to Elgin thanking him for having made it possible for him to be the first artist in modern times to exploit the marbles for the benefit of fine art. Even though West was thought by some to be venerable, it was obvious by his actions that he still needed to appear the first or the best, even when it was unjustified and at the expense of others.

West then attempted to have his letter to Elgin published in an academic periodical. In the academy, a group of academicians who normally supported him deemed what West had written as being incorrect and too full of false self-promotion. They blocked the letter from publication.

CHAPTER 22

Death of a King

In 1764, four years after his marriage to Queen Charlotte, young King George III suffered a relatively mild attack of porphyria that caused him some mental confusion for a brief period. Porphyria is an incurable hereditary disease, which in the eighteenth-century was not well recognized nor its causes understood.

Some twenty-five years later, in the summer of 1788, porphyria still remained little understood when the king suffered his first serious attack. Consequently, for six months, he endured the usual barbaric "cures" to no avail, and by early fall he was slipping into madness. Only a few at court would acknowledge his true condition, until in November 1788 at dinner one day, the king suddenly turned violent. He rose from the table and in a delirium of rage seized the Duke of York, his favorite son, and hurled him against the wall. He was declared insane and physically restrained. By February 1789, he had regained mental and physical health.

Late in his reign, it was said about court that the king admitted that although he disliked Copley, he regretted that he had, except for portraiture, confined his patronage solely to West. But then it was too late to make a change. Copley was losing his skill and the king his health. By 1806 the king's eyesight was so bad that it became fruitless for him to attend academy exhibitions. The king's behavior when he met someone was unpredictable. He was again showing signs of mental derangement said to have been brought on by the death of his favorite daughter, Princess Amelia. In early 1811, the king wisely granted the establishment of a regency, and the Prince of Wales became Royal Regent for the remainder of his father's life, after which he became King George IV. King George IV did not provide West a royal stipend.

As the king's porphyria worsened, he became progressively insane and blind, and suffered great pain from rheumatism. By the end of 1811 until his death in 1820, he lived in isolation at Windsor, needing to be restrained by a straightjacket for much of that time.

CHAPTER 23

West's Family and Apotheosis

y the spring of 1806, Elizabeth, the mother of West's two sons, had suffered two strokes and was suffering through the terminal stages of acute paralysis. She had suffered for many years of such complaints, and they had become progressively worse. She complained to a colleague of her husband that when she first told him that she wanted to go to a spa in Bath to take a cure, he said there was no money to do it. Subsequently, money was found, and they did go to Bath. There, she experienced a little relief, but on return to their residence, her complaints returned. She said that she could barely crawl about their residence. The doctor attending to her medical needs opined that West's painting was bad for Mrs. West, as the smell of white paint brought on her frequent paralytic complaints. He also said that West did not seem to be affected by what might happen in the future, in that he felt only for the present.

Elizabeth also complained that West failed to prepare their two sons for a good future. There is no evidence that they received any college education. Apparently, their function in life was to serve their father. They were used and treated as studio assistants, and were paid as such. They had come to dislike and then resent their situation—Raphael in particular. He had turned into a "party animal" by age nineteen. Reportedly, Raphael felt that if he were free of his father and received £100 a year, he would better apply himself to the art of painting. This did not happen. In 1795, when the Prince of Wales, who would become King George IV, offered West a military commission for Raphael, who was then about twenty-seven, West declined the royal offer. West justified his response by saying that he would not have money sufficient to provide an annual allowance that would enable Raphael to live with other officers in a suitable manner.

In 1797, Raphael married Maria Siltso, the daughter of a farmer, much to the displeasure of his parents. West conceived the idea to send the newly married couple to America, hopeful that they might make his land investment there agriculturally and financially productive. In August 1800, the couple departed for America. It quickly became apparent that Raphael was unfit for the task and Maria unsuitable to manage on the rugged American frontier. Being unsuccessful, they returned to London. Thus, West did not get the supplemental income for which he had hoped. However, West was pleased with his other daughter-in-law, whom West, Junior, married. She was a young lady of refinement who became the mistress of the West household after Mrs. West died.

In December 1806, West, at age sixty-eight, had reclaimed the presidency of the Royal Academy. Even then he could not resist putting himself first and putting down his rival Copley, who was in ill health. While cleaning paintings for Lord Grosvenor, West asserted that Copley's *The Death of Chatham* would have been crude had he not intervened and shown him how to paint a dying man.

West became concerned about how he might be remembered after death at a time when his reputation was rapidly declining. So he hired an unsuccessful hack writer from Scotland to write and publish a biography of his life. No one knows for sure why he chose the thirty-eight-year-old John Galt. Most likely it was because Galt knew very little about West and promised he would tell his life story the way West wanted it told. There was no public record to contradict or constrain West. By 1815, West and Galt were hard at work on the "biography." The following year, the first of the two volume *The Life, Studies and Works of Benjamin West, Esquire* was published. West insisted on carefully correcting the manuscript of the first volume. Nearly all the last proofs of the second volume were submitted to him for approval on his deathbed. Galt wrote the apotheosis West wanted, that is, to be remembered almost in a divine light as a great artist. West's puffing was outrageous.

The second volume was published shortly after West's death in 1820. Although the two volumes survived as biography for more than a century and a half, scholars came to realize that both volumes contained many inaccuracies and exaggerations, and Galt's two volumes came to be dismissed as largely fictional.

West completely ignored the last wish of his wife Elizabeth, who died in 1814. She wanted her grave next to her husband's. This did not happen. Instead, West prearranged a grand burial for himself. He died in 1820 but was not interred until baptismal issues raised by the Anglican church authorities were resolved. Almost three weeks after his death, he was buried with great pomp and ceremony in St. Paul's Cathedral, London.

When West died, he left everything to his two sons except, of course, that which belonged to the king and remained in West's studios. Among those paintings were the religious paintings intended for the Windsor chapels but never hung. The estate was valued to be some £100,000, with debts of about £11,000 and very little cash. In 1826, Raphael, without consulting his brother, spent what cash they did have on enlarging their father's studios so that all of West's work that they had inherited could be placed on exhibition simultaneously and, hopefully, sold quickly. They were unsuccessful. Then they tried to persuade the United States Government to buy what was in the exhibition as the foundation for an American national gallery. But that effort failed. Copley's son, then of some importance, tried to persuade the English government to buy some of West's large pictures, but the government was not interested. Copley, Junior, even went so far as to offer Raphael a post, the best for which he was qualified. But Raphael declined, saying the post was not sufficiently worthy for him to accept.

In the end, West's artistic work was sold at auction. When the two brothers had completely consumed their inheritance, they pleaded for charity from the Royal Academy. They did receive some. Nothing else appears to be known about them.

CHAPTER 24

Copley's Family

s late as 1804, Copley was still receiving public praise for his portraits, but by 1810, at the age of seventy-two, physical weakness, mental impairment, and melancholia took over his life, as did extreme anxiety. Copley was anxious that his residence at 25 George Street, Hanover Square, to which he had moved his family in 1783, would have to be sold, it being highly mortgaged. Nonetheless, he soldiered on, continuing to paint narratives, although unsuccessfully. A tragic figure, he suffered a major stroke in August of 1815 and died peacefully that September. He was buried unpretentiously near London in the Hutchinson family tomb at Croydon Church.

The Hutchinsons and Copleys had been friends since the time Hutchinson was governor of Massachusetts. At the time of his father's death, Copley Jr. was already a successful lawyer, but his father would not know to what level of eminence his son would eventually rise.

Copley Jr. was born in Boston in May 1772. He was fortunate. He had a father not only ambitious for himself, but also ambitious for his son. Copley provided him with not only a primary education, but also the best private secondary school education available. Copley Jr. was a serious student and excelled to such an extent that, as he approached the completion of his studies, his master the Reverend Dr. Horne wrote a glowing report about him to a friend at Trinity College. Consequently, in July 1790, at the age of eighteen, Copley Jr. passed through the gates of Trinity College, Cambridge, where he earned a bachelor degree. By 1795, he was elected a Fellow of Trinity College. Fellows were responsible for maintaining the college as a place for serious learning. That position carried with it not only academic recognition, but also provided a stipend that in young Copley's situation reduced somewhat the economic assistance that he needed from his father. By then, he had also been appointed a traveling bachelor, which brought with it a £100 yearly stipend and free shelter for three years, with the provision that while away from Cambridge, he would report, in Latin, his travel activities and what he had learned from them.

Copley Jr. chose to go to America and arrived there in January of 1796. His first concern was the legal problem regarding the family real estate on Beacon Hill. Unfortunately, when regiments of British troops had occupied Boston, the Copley estate was fortified. In that process, fences that defined the estate were destroyed. When the war with Great Britain ended, Copley Sr. made a big mistake. He placed the care of his real estate in the hands of an agent who, without obtaining authorization from him, disposed of the property for an amount Copley Sr. thought too little. Although Copley Jr. had already started legal studies at Cambridge, he retained Bostonian legal counsel. Their advice was that the best thing for his father to do was to settle the matter out of court because of the possibility that in-court proceedings could declare Copley Sr. an alien and thus deny him ownership of the property. Copley, Jr., communicated this legal advice to his father, which Copley Sr. would reluctantly accept some years later. After completing his business in Boston, the younger Copley toured America. He was welcomed wherever he went, from calling on George Washington at Mount Vernon, Virginia, to meeting chieftains of Indian tribes.

When he returned to England, Copley Jr. earned the honor of being declared second best wrangler, or debater, at Cambridge. His study of law continued, and in his last term at Cambridge, after paying a fee, he was awarded a master's degree. He was then admitted to the Bar in June of 1804, soon after he had represented his father's interest in the Knatchbull arbitration. When his father died, Copley Jr., still a bachelor, took on full responsibility for the care of his mother and spinster sister, Mary. Over a period of four years, he paid off his father's debts and began to refurbish the Copley residence.

He met and married the perfect political wife, Sarah Garay, a very beautiful and highly intelligent widow of an officer who had died in the Battle of Waterloo when Napoleon was finally defeated and sent into permanent exile. After his marriage, Copley moved his mother and spinster sister to a fine and comfortable home about eight miles outside of London. Then the newlyweds moved into the Copley family residence on George Street and made it grand again.

Among the paintings, studies, sketches, and other materials that were left in his father's studio, a great prize awaited Copley Jr.: *The Death of Major Peirson*. His father had found the money in 1805 to buy it back from the print merchant Boydell, who had commissioned it. In later years, during a visit to the Copley residence, the Duke of Wellington, who had defeated the French armies in Portugal and Spain, and then Napoleon himself at Waterloo, viewed *The Death of Major Peirson*. He praised it highly and declared it to be the most realistic painting of warfare he had ever seen. Copley Jr., must have been quite moved by this praise for his father's work from a soldier who had seen so much of war. The painting remained in the Copley residence until the son's death. It was then purchased at auction for £1,600 by the National Gallery in London, accompanied by great applause, and later transferred to the Tate Gallery in London. It is considered Copley's finest narrative painting.

Copley Jr., quickly moved up the English political ladder, becoming a member of Parliament. He was knighted and promoted to solicitor general, a level directly below the highest level in the English legal system. In 1827, he brought great honor to the family name. On the advice of the king's prime minister, he was appointed by the king Lord High Chancellor Lyndhurst and raised to the peerage rank of baron. He was the first non-native-born Englishman to become the king's supreme legal officer, a very high office, something akin to the Attorney General of the United States. As Lord High Chancellor, he performed brilliantly. His mother witnessed his rise to eminence before her death at age ninety in 1830.

CHAPTER 25

Summing Up

As young men, John Singleton Copley and Benjamin West sought the same goals: wealth and artistic fame. When they met in London in 1774, West was well on his way to acquiring them. His good luck in being introduced to King George III resulted in an exclusive, lucrative patronage that lasted for about thirty years. His fame derived mainly from his association with King George III and the enviable title bestowed upon him as History Painter to the King. The bulk of his wealth resulted from the king's willingness to pay whatever West charged for the commissioned paintings.

Copley had no such luck. His reputation and fame rested on the fact that he had natural genius and could create great works of art. His ambition to achieve wealth had its ups and downs, due mostly to lack of royal patronage, cavalier treatment by the print makers, and after 1783, West's continuing hostile behavior.

It has been said about King George III that he took a great interest in painting and fancied himself an able art critic. But the passage of time has not confirmed his artistic judgment. The paintings of his favored artist Benjamin West are generally acknowledged as mediocre, and West's enormous studio output has little more than historical value. Other than royal portraiture, West's paintings for the most part are "uninspired pastiches (imitations of other artists) of enormous size."

Unlike his father, King George III, King George IV could recognize in a painting the combination of great creative imagination and artistic skill that separates the extraordinary from the ordinary. He had little regard for West's paintings. Thus, after West's death, he gave all the religious paintings to West's two sons, except for West's two paintings of the Last Supper, one of which he gave to Parliament.

In narrative painting, West never let the difficulty of incorporating accurate historical facts of an event stand in the way of expeditious production. West's paintings of *The Death of General Wolfe* and *William Penn's Treaty with the Indians* are but two examples of his disregard for historical accuracy. In this regard, one should remember that the camera had not yet been invented. Among the reasons artists were important was that they created for their patrons and the public a visual image of an important historical event that was worth recording.

General Wolfe was a heroic officer. Leading his troops into the thick of battle, he was struck in the wrist but continued leading them. He was then hit in the stomach and chest. After issuing his final orders, he died on the battlefield. Such heroic leadership of an English general is not depicted in West's painting, and neither is his death in the turmoil of a raging battle. Of the thirteen figures surrounding Wolfe, who is stretched out far from the battlefield, only six are identifiable; the others are not. And one wonders why a single Indian is there looking upon the general as if he were a curiosity. Compared to Copley's *The Death of Major Peirson*, it is completely lacking in drama and truthfulness. In West's painting of William Penn, Penn is made to look too old, the dress of the Quakers is that of the eighteenth century, not the seventeenth century when the event allegedly took place, and the dress of the Indians is a mixture of authenticity and fabrication.

Copley's narrative paintings are superior to those of West's. Such is seen clearly in *The Victory of Lord Duncan* and *The Death of Major Peirson*. His portraiture is also superior to that of West's. When the English reviewed portraits painted in London during the eighteenth century and chose the five best portrait painters, Copley was one of the five; West was not. Copley left an invaluable gift to the American people—over one hundred paintings of colonial Americans. Today, Copley's art is still admired; West's art enjoys little admiration.

EPILOGUE

Copley triumphed as an artist.
West, the puffer, failed.

ABBREVIATIONS FOR NOTES

E&S: von Effra, Helmut and Staley, Allen, The Paintings of Benjamin West Yale University Press, 1986

MMA: Metropolitan Museum of Art

Prown: Prown, Jules David, John Singleton Copley in England, 1774–1815

Whitley: Whitley, W.T., Artists and Their Friends in England, 1700–1799, Benjamin Blom, 1928 reissued in 1968, volume I & II

TMHS: Letters & Papers of John Singleton Copley and Henry Pelham, 1739–1776, The Massachusetts Historical Society, Boston, 1914

Notes

Chapter 1. Great Expectations

3. "new meaning to the term precocious," MMA Bulletin, Fall 2003, p. 37.

4. "had never seen a work ...,": MMA Bulletin, Fall 2010, p. 41.

8. *that it exceeded any portrait ...*": Whitley Volume I, p. 215.

Chapter 2. Royal Problems

12. *"We demolished the ..."*: TMHS, p. 36.

Chapter 3. Getting There First

18. *"These are much ..."*: E&S, p. 262.

19.*"Until Mr. West exhibits some more striking ..."*: E&S, p. 262.

21. *"not very fine"*: E&S, p. 180.

Chapter 5. Yankee London Bound

28. *"West was making great progress ..."*: TMHS, p. 55.

Chapter 6. Copley Meets West

33. *"fine picture"*: E&S, p. 213.

"There is too little concern ...": Ibid.

35. *described as cardboard-like ...*: Millar, Oliver, *The Later Georgian Pictures in the Collections of Her Majesty the Queen*, Phaeton Press, Ltd, London, 1969, Volume II, xviii.

Chapter 7. To Italy and Return

42. *"a perfect Master ..."*: Prown, p. 252.

47. *"I do not want ..."*: Dobree, Bonamy, ed., *The Letters of King George III*, Cassell & Company, Ltd., London, 1968 (first published in 1935) p. 106-107.

48. *"Left behind were ..."*: Steele, Matthew Forney, *American Campaigns*, Combat Forces Press, Washington, D.C., 1951, Volume I, p. 13.

Chapter 8. What Next

54. *"a painter in it ..."*: Graves, Algernon, *The Royal Academy of Arts: A Complete Dictionary of Contributors and Their Work from Its Foundation in 1769 to 1904*, Henry Graves and Co. Ltd. 1905, republished by S.R. Publishers Ltd. and Kingsmead Reprints 1970, volume II p. 63.

Chapter 10. Copley Surprises

62. *" The painting received ..."*: Prown, p. 267, footnote 17.

Chapter 12. Parting of Ways

74. *"for prices that ..."*: Solkin, David H., *Painting for Money*, *The Paul Mellon Center for the Studies of British Art*, Yale University Press, 1993, p. 180-181; Note 52, p. 291.

74. *" excelled West in portraiture and rivaling ..."*: Alberts, Robert C., *Benjamin West: A Biography*, Houghton Mifflin Company, Boston 1978, p.155.

75. *" Critical reviews were ..."*: Prown, Volume II p. 307.

Chapter 13. An Angry Young Man

79. *The Three Youngest Daughters of George III.* Roberts, Jane, ed. *The Royal Collection Treasures.* Royal Collection Publications and Scala Publishers Limited, 2008, p. 54.

79. *"felt to be not only cruel and in poor taste"*: Alberts, Robert C. *Benjamin West: A Biography*, Houghton Mifflin Co., Boston 1978, p.172.

79. " Hoppner suggested that ...": Ibid., p. 173.

Chapter 14. A Sneaky Action

82. *"a most beautiful picture"*: Hilles and Daghlian, ed., *Walpole's Anecdotes of Painting in England*, Yale University Press, New Haven, Volume 5, p. 14.

84. *"by the acre"*: E&S, p. 236.

Chapter 15. For Shame, Mr. West

95. " *£36,000 for the Walpole collection"*: Massie, Robert, *Catherine the Great*, Random House, New York, 2011 p. 522

Chapter 16. A Coronation

99. *"not on my part ..."*: Alberts, Robert. *Benjamin West: A Biography*, Houghton Mifflin Company, Boston, 1978 p. 194.

Chapter 19. Loss of Favor

115. *"West rushed to the Louvre ..."*: Alberts, Robert, *Benjamin West: A Biography*, Houghton Mifflin Company, Boston, 1978, p. 270.

Chapter 20. West Has Problems

123. *"West certainly knew nothing of portrait painting ..."*: E&S, p. 493.

Chapter 24. Copley's Family

142. *"The Duke of Wellington ..."*: Prown, p. 302.

Chapter 25. Summing Up

146. *"uninspired pastiches of enormous size..."*: Luhrs, Kathleen, ed., *American Paintings in the Metropolitan Museum of Art*, The Metropolitan Museum of Art in Association with Princeton University Press, 1994. v.I p. 65.

A SELECTIVE BIBLIOGRAPHY

Abrams, Ann Uhry, *The Valiant Hero, Benjamin West and Grand-Style History Painting*, Smithsonian Institution Press, 1985.

Alberts, Robert C. *Benjamin West: A Biography*, Houghton Mifflin Co., 1978.

Evans, Dorinda, *The Genius of Gilbert Stuart*, Princeton University Press, Princeton, New Jersey, 1999.

Fenton, James, *School of Genius: A History of the Royal Academy of Arts*, Royal Academy Publications, Harry N. Abrams, Inc. New York, 2006.

Goodman, Elise, ed. *Art and Culture in the Eighteenth Century: New Dimensions and Multiple Perspectives*, University of Delaware Press, Newark, 2001

Groseclose, Barbara, *Nineteenth-Century American Art*, Oxford University Press, New York, 2000.

Gilbert, Stuart, *Portraitist of the Young Republic*, National Gallery of Art, Washington and Museum of Art, Rhode Island School of Design, 1967.

Hibbert, Christopher, *George III*, Viking of Penguin Books, Ltd.,1998.

Klayman, Richard, *America Abandoned: John Singleton Copley's American Years, 1738-1774*, Lanham, New York, 1983.

Lee, Dennis, *Lord Lyndhurst: The Flexible Tory*, University Press of Colorado, Niwot, Colorado, 1994.

McLanathan, Richard, *Gilbert Stuart*, Harry N. Abrams, Inc., 1986.

Metropolitan Museum of Art, New York, *John Singleton Copley in America*, Harry N. Abrams, Inc., New York, 1995.

Neff, Ballew, *John Singleton Copley in England*, Merrell Holberton, London, 1995.

Prown, Jules David, *John Singleton Copley in England, 1774-1815*, and *John Singleton Copley in America, 1738-1774*, volumes I and II, Harvard University Press, Cambridge, Massachusetts, 1966.

Rebora, Carrie, et. al., *John Singleton Copley in America*, The Metropolitan Museum of Art, Harry N. Abrams, New York, 1995.

Sellers, Charles Coleman, *Patience Wright: American Artist and Spy in George III's London*, Wesleyan University Press, Middletown, Connecticut, 1976.

Vaughan, William, *British Painting, The Golden Age*, Thames and Hudson, New York, 1999.

Von Erffa, Helmut, and Allen Staley, *The Paintings of Benjamin West*, Yale University Press, New Haven, 1986.

WHERE PAINTINGS BY JOHN COPLEY, GILBERT STUART, AND BENJAMIN WEST MAY BE ON VIEW

Paintings by Copley:

Portrait of Elizabeth Greenleaf: Metropolitan Museum of Art, New York City.

Boy with a Squirrel: Museum of Fine Arts, Boston.

Mrs. Gage: Timken Museum of Art, San Diego, California.

The Copley Family: National Gallery of Art, Washington, DC

Watson and the Shark: Museum of Fine Arts, Boston.

The Death of Chatham: Tate Britain, London.

Charles I Demanding the Five Impeached Members of the House of Commons: Boston Public Library, Boston.

The Death of Major Peirson: Tate Britain, London.

The Three Youngest Daughters of George III: The Royal Collection, London.

Paintings by Stuart:

Portrait of John Copley: National Portrait Gallery, London.

Portrait of Benjamin West: National Portrait Gallery, London.

The Skater: National Gallery of Art, Washington, D.C.

Paintings by Benjamin West:

Portrait of Jane Morris: Chester County Historical Society, West Chester, Pennsylvania.

Agrippina Landing at Brundisium with the Ashes of Germanicus: Philadelphia Museum of Art, Philadelphia, Pennsylvania.

Self-Portrait with Raphael West: Yale Center for British Art, New Haven, Connecticut.

The Death of General Wolfe: National Gallery of Canada, Ottawa.

William Penn's Treaty with the Indians: Pennsylvania Academy of Fine Arts, Philadelphia.

St. Paul Shaking off the Viper: The Royal Naval College, Greenwich, England.

Death on a Pale Horse: Pennsylvania Academy of Fine Arts, Philadelphia.